POLIS
IN DEFENCE
OF THE BRITISH ISLES
1939-1945

POLISH FORCES IN DEFENCE OF THE BRITISH ISLES 1939-1945

Edited by
Eugenia Maresch

Papers from the
"Home Front Recall" Conference
to commemorate the 60th Anniversary
of the end of the II World War
organised by the
Federation of Poles in Great Britain

London 17 July 2005

Published in 2006
By
Federation of Poles in Great Britain

Copyright
Federation of Poles in Great Britain
P.O.S.K.
240 King Street London W6 ORF

Acknowledgements
We should like to express our gratitude to
The Polish Institute and Sikorski Museum in London
for the use of their photographs.
Witold Leitgeber for quotations from his book
It Speaks for Itself 1946
And especially
'Home Front Recall', Lottery Fund
for their generous support.

ISBN 0 9543217 0 7

Printed by Veritas Foundation Publication Centre
London

Contributors

Jan Ciechanowski. Prof. Emeritus Thames Valley University, eminent historian and author of *The Warsaw Uprising* and many notable articles.

Teresa Skinder Suchcitz. PhD in History, teacher by profession, prodigious writer on military history in Polish periodicals.

Michael Smith. Journalist, former Defence Correspondent of the daily Telegraph, author of several books on Intelligence.

David List. Researcher, specialist writer and broadcaster on war and military matters, member of BBC History Unit.

Zbigniew Wawer. PhD in History, lecturer, producer and director of documentary films. Lives and works in Poland

Andrzej Suchcitz. PhD in History, writer and keeper of Archives at the Polish Institute & Sikorski Museum.

Eugenia Maresch. Scientist by profession, historian by inclination. Secretary of the Council of Archival Heritage. Member of the Anglo-Polish Historical Committee.

Contents

Preface

POLAND'S CONTRIBUTION to the defeat of Germany was characterised by determination and perseverance. Despite the initial defeat in September 1939, the Poles managed to muster and form five armies – four of them in exile: in France in 1939, then in the summer of 1940 in the United Kingdom (after the capitulation of France). The other two were formed in the USSR, after Soviet Russia had joined the alliance against Germany in 1941. One of these armies, under the command of Gen. Władysław Anders fought alongside the British Army in Italy. The other was communist led and fought alongside the Red Army against the Germans on the Eastern front, driving the Germans back to Berlin. The fifth Polish Army was an underground army with over 300,000 sworn-in troops who fought so fearlessly in occupied Poland. For the entire period of the war, there was also a "silent front" – the Polish Intelligence Service, which co-operated with the British Secret Service (SIS) from the very beginning of the war to its conclusion. In all, some two million Poles, men and women, served in various Polish military forces, some in the regular army, and others in the underground formations. In the final stages of the war, there were some 600,000 regular Polish troops fighting on all the European fronts (army, air force and navy).

In the first days of war, a destroyer flotilla of the Polish Navy avoided the onslaught of bombing by slipping away to join the Royal Navy in Rosyth. The war at sea against the U-boats began in earnest. Polish bomber crews and above all the fighter squadrons flew alongside their British comrades in arms, taking part in the decisive Battle of Britain. The newly formed

Polish Army units stationed in Scotland took their posts along the stretch of Britain's shores as a shield against the German air raids in expectation of imminent invasion.

This collection of historical essays, presented at a Conference organised by the Federation of Poles in Great Britain on 14 July 2005, bear witness to their gallantry. Determined to restore the freedom and independence of Poland, they fought for the ideals of liberty of others. Yet, in 1945 – with the silent consent of the Western Allies, Poland found itself under the yoke of Soviet communism and the Victory Parade of 1946 was denied them.

It is hoped that this historical account, albeit of necessity short, will serve as a further and valued contribution to the understanding and evaluation of all that was achieved through the participation of our generation in the Second World War.

Ryszard Kaczorowski GCMG

Former President of Poland
residing in London

Foreword

THE FEDERATION OF POLES in Great Britain, for all sorts of reasons, has a long tradition of organising Polish Festivals. This year due to the 60th anniversary of the end of the war and to commemorate their settlement in this country, the Festival together with other events had to have a wider dimension. On July 4th, in the splendour of the Grand Locarno Rooms of the Foreign and Commonwealth Office the Foreign Secretaries of Great Britain Mr Jack Straw and Poland's Mr Adam Rotfeld, launched the Report of the Joint Anglo-Polish Historical Committee, *Intelligence co-operation between Poland and Great Britain in the II World War* vol.1. Later, General Sir Michael Walker, Chief of Defence Staff, in the presence of General Czesław Piátas, Chief of General Staff of the Polish Armed Forces at a ceremony in Lancaster House, presented British War Medal 1939-45 to Mrs. Janina Sylwestrzak. She received it on behalf of her late father Marian Rejewski (1905-1980), one of the three Polish mathematicians who first cracked the codes of the Enigma, German cipher machine. With impending war, unable to continue, the Poles passed on their secret information and copies of Enigma to their British and French allies in July 1939.

The overall contribution of the Polish Armed Forces to the Allied victory in WW II was immense. It provided the fourth largest army fighting Germany, as well as the one who fought for the longest time. It would take several volumes to describe at any length the contribution of Polish Forces at the battles of Narvik and Tobruk, at Monte Cassino, Falaise and Breda, of the Polish Parachute Brigade at Arnhem, of the Polish Navy in the battle of the Atlantic and Merchant Navy in convoying.

The crucial role the Polish Air Force played in the victorious Battle of Britain and later in the bombing raids over Germany is already well documented. Poland's Home Army was the largest and best organised resistance force in occupied Europe. The importance of the Home Army partisan activity, the Warsaw uprising, the acts of sabotage on German supply lines, as well as the constant supply of intelligence material should not be underestimated.

The Polish Festival started on 14th July with a Day Conference, organised and chaired by Mrs Eugenia Maresch, to whom all credit is due. It was enhanced by a display of museum exhibits, lent by the Polish Institute and Gen. Sikorski Museum and a photographic exhibition prepared by Mr Grzegorz Stachurski. The Conference was entitled "Home Front Recall", after its benefactor, without whose financial assistance this splendid event would not have been possible. In the conference we confined ourselves to a fairly narrow field - the Polish contribution to the defence of the British Isles. To give this relatively unknown subject its proper importance we assembled a group of distinguished British and Polish historians, each a specialist in his chosen field. This little volume of their contributions will shed light on yet another chapter of our recent history.

Finally, in separate events those few Polish Combatants who survived, at long last took part in a special parade commemorating allied victory of World War II, something shamefully denied to them 60 years ago. Also remembered was the incredible struggle for freedom by the Solidarność movement brought democracy not just to Poland, but eventually to the rest of Eastern Europe and signalled the demolition of the Berlin wall, leaving Europe without barriers. The help, which Solidarność received from the British people, the Trade Union

Movement and the British Government has been appreciated and noticed.

Presently, Poland is a full member of the NATO and the European Union. Hopefully this Alliance will go a long way in building a new and prosperous Europe.

Jan Mokrzycki

Chairman of the Federation of Poles in Great Britain.

Introduction

"I and my peoples in this country and overseas are filled with admiration for the courage and tenacity of the Polish people. We are proud to have at our side in the defence of these Islands the heroic Polish Army, Air Force and Navy, which have covered themselves with glory during the last twelve months. The stirring feats of Polish aviators in the air battles now proceeding over England are bringing new honour to Polish arms. I share the conviction of the final defeat of the tyranny now menacing Europe and I look with confidence to the restoration of Polish independence and of the liberties of Europe."

(H.M. King George VI, 4 September 1940)

I OFTEN BROWSE through historical books, just to find out if there are any references to the contribution made by the Polish Armed Forces to the war effort during the Second World War. Usually not a great deal is recorded, unless written by a Pole in the Polish language in connection with an anniversary. This year in particular, even the British media avoided reappraisals of the Poles, who stood alongside the British in defence of these Isles. However, I am delighted that in recent years excellent books have been published, written by British and American authors and that this little volume of papers given at a Conference to commemorate the 60 anniversary of the II World War, hopefully, will expound the subject further. My role as the organiser of the Conference and editor of this volume is purely academic. In my summary, I have chosen to write about different aspects on the same theme. It is intended to be an addendum to the already comprehensive articles of individual authors.

Let me start with the issue of Anglo-Polish relations, concerning mutual defence against Germany. By signing an agreement on the eve of the outbreak of war, both our countries were obliged to assist each other in 'their hour of need'. The Poles were naturally anxious over the delay in declaring war on Germany by Britain and France. Chamberlain's unsolicited guarantee of March 1939 to defend the Polish frontiers did not result in practical military help when the time came .By clear thinking, the Polish Naval Command ordered three of her destroyers: GROM, BŁYSKAWICA and BURZA to leave Gdynia for British ports while there was time. Two submarines WILK and ORZEŁ were to follow to take part in the 'twilight war' at sea, after a great feat of escape and evasion from the enemy. The Admiralty welcomed this small but brave and determined Polish Navy. They knew that their resources of fighting the German U-boats were limited, as was the defence capability of British warships from enemy air attacks. The Royal Navy had to concentrate upon the strategy of adopting a convoy system to protect the shipping lifeline of the country bringing food and war equipment.

Meanwhile in Poland, the Army was fully engaged in battling the advancing Germans. Keenly observed by Maj.Gen.Carton de Wiart, head of the British Military Mission in Poland, through Capt. F.T. Davies, he sent a report to Maj.Gen.Beaumont-Nesbitt, Director of Military Intelligence at the War Office in London, in which he expressed great anxiety over the seriousness of the situation. With German supremacy completely neutralizing Polish counter attacks, Carton de Wiart requested urgent and immediate air support to ward off the attacks. He declared that the French Military Mission was of the opinion that the flying distance to Poland – was feasible and stressed absolute urgency to permit supplies of war materials to reach Poland.

In Davies' words, the delay of 48 hours of the British declaration of war had caused the greatest mistrust of British intentions, which would continue to exist until positive action is taken by the British forces to relieve pressure on the Eastern front. Furthermore, the dropping of pamphlets by British bombers in Germany has only caused considerable disdain in Poland and served no useful purpose. Wiart was desperate to inform the War Office that British intentions were interpreted merely as a waiting game until Poland is completely overrun – when some sort of back stage peace would be agreed with Hitler. The report of the Military Mission went unheeded. The truth came out after the war, when Winston Churchill in his book *The Second World War, The Gathering Storm*, wrote that the French Government requested Britain to abstain from air attack on Germany, as it might have provoked a retaliation upon their war factories, which were unprotected and Britain "*had to contain herself to dropping pamphlets to rouse the Germans to a higher morality. France and Britain remained impassive while Poland was in a few weeks destroyed or subjugated by the whole might of the German war machine*". No comments are needed to this profound statement.

Although the feeling towards the British began with distrust, events caused this to change to one of hope. In spite of the alliance with Poland, Romania was frightened by Hitler into strict neutrality and started to intern thousands of Polish soldiers who crossed their border en route to France and Britain. With the help of some Romanians and assistance from allied embassy staff, the majority of airmen and soldiers reached their destination, most to France, others to Syria. After the fall of France in June 1940, when the Polish government and its forces had to seek shelter in Great Britain, loyalty and appreciation had grown towards her, as only she offered salvation to Poland. The words of the then Prime Minister Winston Churchill in his letter to Gen. W. Sikorski, expresses the essence of feelings between the two allies:

"I was very glad to see the Polish forces in Scotland. Their smart and resolute bearing convinced me that when the call for action comes, they would confirm the reputation for soldierly and audacious bravery, which they and their comrades have already won on the battlefields of Poland, France and Norway. Poland had shed her blood in that same cause of Right and Freedom for which we in England are fighting and now in the hour of her misfortune we watch with admiration the indomitable will of her sons, wherever they may be to fight on till the enemy has been defeated. Though their country be trampled underfoot by the oppressor, the Polish people who have struggled so long and so honourably for their natural existence and independently will in the end achieve their hearts' desire."

The indomitable will of a new generation of Poles, who had grown up between the wars in an independent Poland, was truly remarkable. They were enthusiastic and capable soldiers, not to be outdone by the military prowess of France or Britain. Polish universities and polytechnics were producing talented engineers and mathematicians, who became the envy of the western allies. The best example of innovative research was undertaken by the Polish cryptologists, especially Rejewski who broke the codes of the Enigma machine in 1932, by using mathematical permutations. By presenting a copy of Enigma and sharing its secret configuration with French and British Intelligence Services in 1939, the Poles advanced the British production of their 'bombe' by at least a year. Ralph Erskine, in *Intelligence and National Security* vol.3 1988, stated:

"It is difficult to see how, without Polish contribution (which indirectly helped all Bletchley Park's work on plugboard Enigma to get off the ground), Hut 8 could have solved Triton

[German naval signals] effectively before August 1943 – and perhaps not even then."

Numerous inventions were the bi-product of creative minds of engineers and technicians. Some projects were fully developed before the war, others were in various stages of development. Among most prominent were: the tank periscope, mine detector, miniature radios and fuses. Some Poles branched off to radar experiments for directional finding and signal interception as well as submarine antennae, which were installed on convoy ships. All these inventions were placed by the Polish Government at the disposal of HMG for the duration of war. Under UK law, the rights belonged to the British by reason of the Polish Units being attached to the British Forces.

The British Secret Intelligence Service (SIS) started to co-operate with its Polish counterpart, by running a special Polish Section, headed by Cmdr. Wilfred Dunderdale (A4, known as 'Wilski'). He handled liaison with the Polish Intelligence Service (II Bureau Polish General Staff) headed from 1941 by Col. Stanisław Gano. The intelligence gathered by the Polish services, chiefly by the soldiers of the Polish Underground Army, known as Home Army, was passed to SIS, which after evaluation passed onto the relevant Ministries and Allied Commands. One stark example among many was found in a War Office 'Appreciation File' dated 24 January 1940, in connection with information passed by the Poles, regarding Hitler's plans for England's invasion. It stated that:

"A great offensive against England is planned by the Germans in three phases: aerial attack, setting mine fields and preparing parachute regiments at Weiningen near Stuttgart". The information was passed onto the Joint Intelligence Committee, but was totally ignored with comments that: " the Polish Intelligence is comfortingly unreliable". Precious time was wasted in preparing the Island's defences.

By the time the Battle of Britain began in July 1940, there were three thousand seven hundred men of the Polish Air Force who had been evacuated to Great Britain. Out of these 2,230 men were already incorporated in the RAF and probably, over two thousand more were still scattered in different camps with the Army troops. They were to be placed under the orders of the Allied High Command as independent Allied troops but grouped together under a General Polish Command. For most Polish soldiers and airmen, this was going to be their third campaign within a year. The fighter pilots had already to their credit 129 downed German planes in Poland and 51 in the French campaign.

The RAF Command at first was very cautious in recognising the strength and ability of the Polish airmen. They did not appreciate that the Polish pilots were older and more experienced than the new British recruits with only several hours of flying. What perhaps convinced them most to change their minds was the fact that the Poles brought with them their ground crews of mechanics and other support staff, who were the mainstay of all operations undertaken by Polish Fighter and Bomber Squadrons. With this in mind, the British plan was to form at least four wings of fighters, four of bombers and two wings of so called co-operation planes with suitable reserves of flying and auxiliary personnel. All that the Poles needed was to become accustomed to using the throttle of the Hurricanes and Spitfires and learn the English language.

8 August 1940 was the day when German Luftwaffe intensified their fierce attack upon Britain, sowing death and destruction intending to wipe out the RAF and their airfields. The Polish Squadrons 302 and 303 joined the Battle on 19 of August to defend aerodromes on the coast and inland. A number of Polish pilots, flying as individual members of RAF Squadrons had already scored successes in the air. 7 September was a particular momentous day when the Polish Squadrons

along with the RAF faced 500 German machines targeting London. The Poles downed 16 planes with a further 4 probable. Air combat was undertaken each day with the greatest of all air battles taking place on 15 September 1940, when the entire Big Wing including the Polish Squadrons, under the command of S/Ldr Douglas Bader took to the sky, not once but twice to face 400 bombers as they came up from the Kent coast towards London. In his captivating talk at the Conference, which unfortunately I am unable to present in this book, Adam Zamoyski, has drawn a vivid picture of the 146 Polish airmen who participated in the Battle of Britain. For interested readers, may I recommend his splendid book - *The Forgotten Few. The Polish Air Force in the World War II*, London 2004.

In June 1940, after the Dunkirk evacuation in which Polish naval and merchant ships, escorted by Polish pilots, Britain was in a frantic state to prepare the defenceless Islands for an invasion, which at that time appeared to be inevitable. The state of Scottish defences where a possible secondary invasion was expected was very poor. Only two batteries of anti-aircraft guns were placed each at Aberdeen, Peterhead, Montrose and North Berwick. There were no defences at Scapa Flow, which could have led into a disaster. Armed only with experience gained during the devastating campaigns in Poland, France and Norway, various units of the Polish Army evacuated from France started to land at British ports.

The British Army Commander Brigadier Major T.L. Binney of the General Staff Scottish Command considered the fighting value of these Polish units very highly provided they were kept as one large operational unit and are suitably armed and equipped as the British. It must be said that the Poles surpassed themselves. They were adaptable to the new conditions of life in the field; they were mobile and experienced in operational warfare especially in anti-tank weaponry as well as building anti-tank barrages.

Most extraordinary was the creation of armoured trains consisting of small tank engines with cattle trucks in front and rear. A slightly amusing operation, with uncanny resemblance to TV series "Dad's Army'. Luckily the elderly officers did not encounter the enemy and the whole exercise proved useful to bolster the defences of the southern and eastern coasts of Britain.

Thus, Scotland became home for thousands of Polish troops and the Glasgow region a rallying point for a steady influx of soldiers marching the streets lined with bewildered Scots. Unfamiliar towns and villages: Crawford, Biggar, Douglas, Dunns and many others. Unfamiliar language and bad weather had its toll. Billeted in tents without beds, with constant rain and fog, they awaited eagerly to be posted to proper camps and given proper arms, longing to take action against Germany without much delay. But the time machine was going at a slow pace. Months went by on yet another reorganisation of the Polish corps, settling in different towns and regions. St Andrews took on the Polish forces with a certain amount of friendliness. When not on manoeuvres, the Poles were used to help the local farmers with gathering the harvest of grain, beetroots and potatoes. The locals thought them gallant and friendly in spite of the fact that they could not communicate. This was soon put right by the Poles offering free rounds of tots of whisky and sign language did the rest. But this state did not last long; troops were on the move again, changing garrisons, building fortifications and setting up barrages and at long last guarding the coasts of the British Isles. In his diary for 25 December 1940, Lt-Col Karol Maresch commander of the 1st Light Artillery Battery over St Andrews described how he spent his first Christmas in Scotland, with Prof. Dickie, his wife and daughter. In the glow of the fireplace he ate the traditional dinner of turkey and plum pudding, which was a totally unknown speciality. The peace and warmth of a happy home, good will and sympathy drained deeply into a Pole's heart. He has lost his home and family and had no news of them. He pondered, how distant were his thoughts in reaching them and how futile were his hopes of seeing a quick victory of the mighty ally.

This truly captivating 'recall of the home front' is one of many facts and figures, which the book contains. It is our fervent hope that it will make the new generation of Poles, scattered throughout the world - extremely proud of.

Eugenia Maresch

Poland and Great Britain 1939-1945

Jan Ciechanowski

> 'Tomorrow I return to France' said Gen. Sikorski gravely to the Prime Minister, 'and I have to face my army. What am I to tell them?'
> 'Tell them', replied Mr. Churchill, 'that we are their comrades in life and in death. We shall conquer together or we shall die together.' They shook hands. 'That handshake' said Gen. Sikorski – 'meant more to me than any treaty of alliance or any pledged word'.
>
> (18 June 1940)

ANGLO-POLISH RELATIONS as well as political and military co-operation, during the Second World War was based on the provisions of Neville Chamberlain's guarantees to Poland of 31 March 1939 and on a pact of unilateral military assistance concluded by London and Warsaw on 25 August 1939. On 31 March the British Prime Minister Neville Chamberlain, told the House of Commons that: " *in the event of any action which clearly threatens Polish independence, and which the Polish Government considered it vital to resist with their national forces, His Majesty's Government would feel themselves bound to lend the Polish Government all support in their power"*. Armed with this assurance, Poland was the first country to confront Hitler's demands of May 1939.

Chamberlain's guarantees constituted a dramatic and extraordinary step in British foreign policy, traditionally shunning any firm commitments to small East European States. By this declaration, Great Britain pledged herself not only in case of unprovoked open aggression, but also in case of a threat to Poland's independence. The conclusion of the Anglo-Polish treaty was immediately announced, as a deterrent to restrain Hitler from starting a war, to make clear to him that an attack on Poland meant war with Great Britain and France. In brief, a war on two fronts, which Hitler tried to avoid. However, from a purely military point of view the British commitments had little practical value, because Great Britain was in no better position than France to render immediate military help to Poland. Nevertheless, the agreement provided a general political framework within which Anglo-Polish relations were conducted in the following years.

From the start, the British did not expect to save Poland's independence; they envisaged that it would be restored only after they had defeated Germany. Indeed even before the outbreak of hostilities, the British and the French believed that nothing could be done to assist Poland. This made Poland's defeat inevitable as only a massive concerted and immediate Anglo-French offensive could have saved her from utter destruction. No such offensive was launched despite Polish expectations and demands. Neither Great Britain nor France planned or considered herself able to furnish Poland with effective military help in the event of German attack. The Anglo-French guarantees to Poland timed at preventing war – deterring Hitler from attacking Poland – not supporting her militarily in the event that war should break out. The British and French declarations of war for the time being were nothing more than diplomatic gestures. The Poles were unaware of these fateful decisions of her Western Allies.

As early as 24 April 1939, the British and French General Staffs had jointly recognised that in the first phase of the war the only offensive weapon, which the Allies could use effectively was the trade embargo. They also had agreed that initially, their major strategy would be defensive. Further, in July 1939 they had decided that the fate of Poland would depend upon the final outcome of the war, and not on Anglo-French ability to relieve pressure at the outset. They knew that they could not open a decisive campaign against Germany in 1939 or 1940. In September 1939, the British Cabinet decided to make plans on the assumption that the war would go on at least for three years. The first year could be only one of preparation. At the early stages of the war the Western Powers planned to avoid an all-out confrontation with Germany, to gain time for the development of their own forces. Instead, they intended to apply a naval blocked which had been so effective during the First World War. In brief, the Western Powers were determined to wage a war of attrition against Germany.

In the second half of 1940, Great Britain stood alone against the Axis powers and kept the faltering anti-German alliance alive. At that time defeated Poland was her main ally, which testifies to the seriousness of the situation. While helping Britain in many ways, the United States was still non-combatant and the Soviet Union was still trying to cultivate good relations with Nazi Germany. Moreover, the British were already trying to improve their relations with the Soviet Union and hoping to persuade the Poles to accept the loss of Eastern Poland as the necessary price of a Polish-Soviet rapprochement. The problem of post-war Polish-Soviet relations and frontiers was one of the most acute and complicated political issues, which the Allies had to face during the Second World War.

After the fall of France in June 1940, when London became the seat of the highest Polish political and military authorities and the remnants of the Polish Armed Forces were stationed in this country, Great Britain assumed a special responsibility for the fate of Poland and became her main ally and protector. Anglo-Polish relations and cooperation were very cordial and fruitful until Hitler's attack on the Soviet Union in June 1941. The entire course of the war changed when Hitler invaded the Soviet Union.

24 Ciechanowski

As Jan Karski rightly put it :

"Overnight, the USSR found itself on the side of Great Britain. Overnight, the problem of Soviet-Polish relations acquired a new significance".

On 19 June 1940 Winston Churchill, newly-appointed British Prime Minister, assured Gen. Władysław Sikorski, his Polish counterpart and the C-in-C, that: *"We are comrades in life and death we shall conquer together, or we shall die together".* The two Prime Ministers shook hands. *"That handshake",* Sikorski said *"meant more to me than any signed treaty or alliance or any pledged word".* In this manner the Anglo-Polish alliance was *"reaffirmed and cemented".* Churchill assured Sikorski that he could count on him *"for ever"* and that Britain *"will keep faith with the Poles".*

In this dramatic, Churchillian style, a very close political and military co-operation started to develop between Great Britain and Poland at a time when both countries were fighting for their very survival and when Germany seemed to be invincible. This Anglo-Polish co-operation was to last for the rest of the war, and although it finished, after Yalta, in a flurry of mutual recrimination, it left a deep imprint on the histories and psyches of both nations. As one German general put it quite recently, *"We Germans know how to start wars but we do no know how to finish them".* Poland and Great Britain were the only two countries which fought against the Third Reich from the very beginning of the Second World War to its – for the majority of Poles – bitter end. Poland was the first country to resist German open aggression and the attack on Poland on 1 September, precipitated the outbreak of the Second World War with all its consequences.

The arrival of Polish troops from France called for the conclusion of Anglo-Polish agreements defining their legal status and jurisdiction in Great Britain. One of the first military agreements was conducted on 18 November 1939. It concerned the stationing of the Polish Navy in British ports for duration of the war and its engagement under the operational control of the British Naval authorities. A similar agreement concluded on 5 August provided for the formation of Polish Air Force units in Great Britain attached to the Royal Air Force. The Anglo-Polish military agreement stated that:

"The Polish Armed Forces (comprising Land, Sea and Air Forces) shall be organized and employed under British command in its character as the Allied High Command, as the Armed Forces of the Republic of Poland allied with the United Kingdom. The pay for the officers and men of the Polish Armed Forces was to be equal to that of the officers and men of corresponding categories in the British Forces. Equipment, supplies and facilities used by the Polish Forces were to be charged to the credit of the Polish Government".

The agreement also stated that all personnel of the Polish land forces will be subject to Polish military law and disciplinary ruling and they will be tried in Polish military courts. A separate agreement was reached in September 1940, under Churchill's supervision provided for a close and fruitful Anglo-Polish intelligence cooperation. In brief, one period of very close Anglo-Polish political and military co-operation ensued which continued until the end of the war. Great Britain assumed special responsibility for the fate of Poland, while the Polish Armed Forces under British command and the Polish resistance movement rendered great services to the common cause.

The role of the Soviet Union was the single most important factor affecting the relations between the Polish, British and American Government during the war years. In Churchill's own words: *"the attitude of Russia to Poland lay at the root of our early relations with the Soviets."* The outbreak of German-Soviet hostilities brought Great Britain respite from an apparently near hopeless situation and inspired most people in German-occupied Europe with new hope of victory. The German attack on the USSR opened new possibilities with regard to Polish-Soviet relations. The fact that both the Soviets and the Poles were fighting against the common enemy made for temporary Polish-Soviet understanding. The British Cabinet played an important part in bringing about a Polish-Soviet rapprochement. From the very beginning of the German-Soviet war Churchill and Roosevelt made great efforts to establish and cultivate good relations with Stalin, and to convince the latter of their goodwill and support.

On 30 July a Polish-Soviet pact was signed by Gen. Sikorski and the Soviet Ambassador, Ivan Maisky in the presence of Churchill and Anthony Eden, the British Foreign Secretary. The treaty provided for the restoration of Polish-Soviet relations, the creation of a Polish Army in the Soviet Union and an amnesty (or rather release from camps and prisons) of all Polish citizens detained in Russia. However, this pact has failed to settle the question of future frontiers between the two countries. During the negotiations leading to the Soviet-Polish treaty both sides laid claims to pre-war eastern Poland. Sikorski's failure to settle the frontier problem in 1941 left open the whole question of the future Polish-Soviet relations, especially in the event of a decisive Soviet victory. Moscow recognized that the Nazi-Soviet agreements of 1939 with regard to Poland had lost their validity.

On 6 December 1941 Japan attacked Pearl Harbor. On 11 December 1941 Germany declared war on America. As a result of these developments the war assumed global dimensions and the Grand Alliance was finally formed. The outbreak of the conflict in the Far East and Anglo-American involvement in it strengthened the role of Russia within the Alliance, has diminished that of Poland. Throughout the war the Red Army bore the main brunt of the struggle against Germany by engaging the bulk of Nazi land-forces on the Eastern Front. America's entry into the war placed her enormous economic, financial and military resources at the disposal of the Allies. Roosevelt considered Stalin as his main ally in the struggle against the Axis Powers.

As the war went on the Polish Armed Forces in the West, which by the end of hostilities were 220,000-strong, took part in some of the most important battles of the war in France, Italy, the Low Countries and Germany. The Poles fought at Narvik, Tobruk Monte Cassino, the Falaise Gap, and Arnhem, they also took part in defense of the British Isles in the Battle of Britain and the Battle of the Atlantic. The Poles, by capturing Monte Cassino opened the way to Rome and by closing the Falaise Gap – opened the way to Paris. During the Battle of Britain, the Polish fighter pilots shot down 15 % of German planes. The famous Polish 303 Squadron alone downed 110 German planes. Shortly after the Battle of Britain, Air Marshal Sir Hugh Dowding, Chief of the Fight Command stated: *"Had it not been for the magnificent performance of the Polish Squadrons 302 and 303 and their unsurpassed gallantry, I hesitate to say that the outcome of the battle would have been the same"*. Sir Archibald Sinclair, British Air Minister, also stressed that the contribution of the Poles made the difference between victory and defeat – *"our shortage of trained pilots"* he emphasized *"would have made it impossible to defeat the German Air Force and so win the Battle of Britain, if the airmen of Poland had not leaped into the breach"*.

Further, the Polish Intelligence Service and the Resistance in Poland provided London with a constant flow of information concerning German military and naval deployments as well as industrial production of new weapons. Recent research undertaken at Polish and British archives, have shown that the Polish Home Army intelligence service had agents who collected information in almost every German armaments factory and ports, in German occupied territories as well as in Poland. The Poles supplied the allies 44 per cent of all intelligence reports received during war.   It should be remembered that it was the Poles who supplied British with a V2 complete rocket engine in the summer of 1944.

Further more, as Prof. M.R.D. Foot has stressed: "Probably the most important service the Poles ever rendered to the anti-Nazi cause was something they did before the war had even begun". On 25 July 1939, in Warsaw, they handed over their top secret of how to break the coded messages of Enigma ciphers plus a replica of the machine, which astounded the British Intelligence Service. This had enormous consequences to the war effort as it allowed the code-breakers at Bletchley Park to read some of the most secret and important German orders and dispositions and distribute them under the code-name Ultra to some of the most senior British and American Operational Commands including the Soviets. To quote Prof. Foot again: *"Some Ultra was of almost unbelievable high quality: operation instructions from Hitler personally sent to his supreme commanders, which now and again were read by his enemies even before they had been got in the hands of their momentarily absent addressees. It all originated with the pre-war Polish Secret Service"*.

There were times, as Sir David Hunt, the war-time Chief of Intelligence to Field Marshall Alexander, told me, when the British commanders got a clearer idea of the situation at the front from the information received from Ultra than from the reports of their subordinates. Recently, the Ultra materials kept at Bletchley Park were made available to researchers in the national Archives, and they are the best proof of their vital importance. In fact, it could be said that Ultra has introduced an "Extra Dimension" into the conduct of the war. From reading these documents one gets the impression that, during the Battle for Normandy and the closing stages of the Battle for the

Atlantic, British and American Commanders knew almost every German move and order. The British passed onto the Russian the German plans and dispositions for the Battle of Kursk, which finally decided the outcome of the war on the Eastern Front. The Polish Government also tried to alert the British and American authorities to the fact that the Germans were consistently destroying Polish and other European Jewry but Victor Cavendish-Bentinck, the wartime head of the Joint Intelligence Committee, considered the reports to be exaggerated. Nonetheless, he fully admitted that in this intelligence game the Poles were the best people by far.

From 1941 onwards the British were supplying the Polish Resistance Movement with airdrops of highly trained personnel, money, arms and equipment for its intelligence, sabotage and diversionary activities. However, the British authorities refused to provide the Polish Home Army with weapons and equipment for its planned "general insurrection" which was to take place at the most crucial moment of the war, with the aim of freeing the country from the Germans and helping the exiled Polish Government to assume power in its own capital. The responsibility for launching such an insurrection was left by the British Cabinet in the hands of the Polish Government. On 5 October 1943 Eden told the British War Cabinet that the question of supplying the Home Army with arms was problematical as such action, could not be undertaken without consulting the Russians, who might be antagonized.

Nevertheless, in the event, and in spite of enormous technical difficulties and the distances involved, the British Government tried to save the ill-fated Warsaw Rising of 1944 by supplying the insurgents with some arms and ammunition from the British bases in Italy. Further, Churchill tried to save Warsaw from utter defeat and destruction by pressing Stalin and Roosevelt to give help to the stricken city.

In fact, only the Russians could have saved Warsaw from complete destruction at the hands of the Germans, by launching an immediate offensive aimed at capturing the Polish capital.   Stalin refused to do this, claiming that military obstacles and supply-difficulties prevented it.   The evidence suggests, however, that his refusal to help Warsaw was a political rather than a military decision, aimed at ensuring German destruction of his Polish opponents.

President Roosevelt was also reluctant to give decisive help to the unfortunate Poles, as he feared that this might upset his relations with Moscow.   At this time, Roosevelt was pursuing what today President Clinton calls *"Russia first"* policy, and his interest in Polish affairs was minimal.   Roosevelt believed that the Big Three should agree *"at the appropriate time"* on a solution of the Polish problem, and impose it on the Poles.   In 1944 Roosevelt already regarded the USSR and Stalin as the main ally, with whom he wished to establish lasting, including post-war, co-operation. Rather naively, Roosevelt believed that if Stalin was well treated by his Western allies - kept satisfied by them, he would respond in kind and so become *"club-bable"*.   At this time there was a feeling in the West, which Churchill to some extent shared, that after all, Stalin was not so bad and that it was only his *"entourage"* which was stopping him from wholehearted co-operation with Washington and London. The idea was to make Stalin a worthwhile member of the Anglo-American *"club"* presided over by the United States, which by then has risen to the rank of a political, economic and military super-power. However, Stalin wanted to become chairman of his own *"progressive club"*, in which there was no place for what he called *"imperialists"* and *"reactionaries"* such as the London Poles. He was determined – after the Red Army's victories at Stalingrad and Kursk – to include Poland and other East European countries in his own *"club"*, regardless of their wishes and aspiration, and there was no question that he would join any club run by the United States, as a co-chairman. By the end of 1943, there were "clubs" in the making, although this fact was obscured by the tug-of-war and the need to defeat the common enemy. Indeed, one of the main problems, which constantly bedeviled Anglo-Polish co-operation, was the state of Polish-Soviet relation, which throughout the entire war were plagued by almost constant political and territorial problems and the question of about 14,000 Polish officers captured by the Red Army in Poland in September 1939, whose disappearance Stalin could never fully explain. In fact the Russians murdered them in the spring of 1940, and this – the Katyn affair – led to a breakup of diplomatic relations between Moscow and the Polish Government in exile on the 25 April 1943, when the Germans discovered the graves. Following the German discovery of the about 4,000 graves in Belorussia, the British felt that the Russians had committed this atrocity, however, they urged the Poles to say as little as possible about it. Churchill believed that the Katyn affair was an embarrassment and *"not one of these matters where absolute certainty is either urgent or desirable"*. He also argued *"There is no use prowling around the three year old graves of Smolensk"*.

British wartime diplomacy aimed at improving relations between Poland and the Soviet Union for the sake of allied unity. Churchill saw Russian treatment of Poland as a touchstone of Anglo-Soviet relations. Both he and Eden devoted a great deal of their time and effort to heal the rift between Poland and the Soviet Union, unfortunately without much success.

It should not be forgotten, that Churchill was one of the three main architects, of the allied victory – without which the continued existence of Poland as a State and Nation would have been impossible – but also of the present-day frontiers and ethnic composition of post-war Poland. In fact, Churchill was the first of the Big Three leaders to make the official suggestion at the Teheran Conference in 1943, that the frontiers of post-war Poland should be shifted 150 miles to the west at the expense of Germany, that the Poles should cede eastern boarders of Poland to the Soviet Union, and that the Germans might be expelled from this newly-drawn Polish State.

Thus, at a stroke, Churchill proposed to move Poland westward into the very heart of Europe, in order to resolve once and for all the centuries-old territorial dispute between Russia and Poland over eastern boarders with its large Ukrainian and Byelorussia minorities. By expelling the German minority they hoped to consolidate the prospects for the durability of the newly proposed Polish frontier in the west.

Although acceptable to Stalin and Roosevelt, this proposal was too radical for the Poles as no Polish leader at the time- neither Gen. Władysław Sikorski, the Polish Prime Minister from 1939 until 1943, nor his successor, Stanisław Mikłajczyk (and these were the two Polish leaders who understood that some territorial concessions were inevitable) were prepared to accept such a drastic solution. The Polish government strongly objected to loosing Wilno and Lwów, the two ancient centers of Polish culture and learning in the eastern provinces of Poland. They argued that by resisting such a drastic solution they were in reality defending Poland's independence. They also feared that if they accepted Churchill's proposals, some compatriots (to whom such ideas were an anathema), at home and abroad would condemn them. Sir Alexander Cadogan the Permanent Under Secretary at the Foreign Office, felt at the time that:

"The Polish Government certainly had a terrible choice before them. They look like choosing to safeguard their won honour at the expense of their country. Whether this is right morally, I don't pretend to say. What are we going to do?"

A typical Polish field chapel in Johnston nr Glasgow 1940, visited by the Scottish children.

Scottish children having a picnic while on a visit to a Polish unit.

Auld Lang Syne

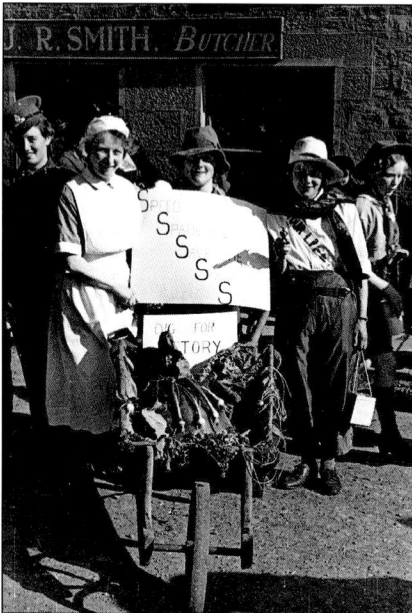

Mrs Stirling and friends collecting for 'War Weapons Week' with the motto 'Speed the Spade and Save the Sailor's Sea', Latham 1941

Lt A. Maszkowski, a teacher of English with his landlady billeted at Haddington 1942

Helping hands at hay making, Scotland 1941

Christmas Dinner with a Scottish family, Edinburgh 1942

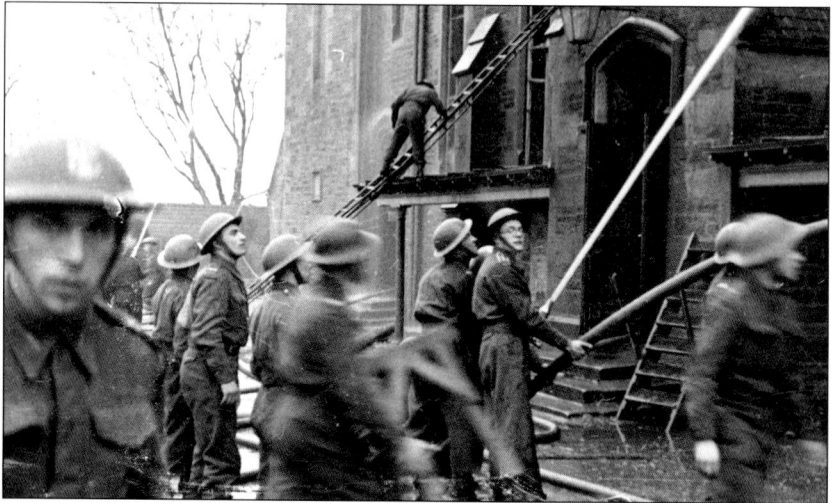

Polish soldiers of the 10 Mounted Rifles Regiment putting out a fire in Forfar 1941

A plane of 304 Polish Coastal Command Squadron on patrol

Barrage balloons

Polish air and ground crew of 300 Squadron with their Wellington

Polish Wing, part of the Tactical Air Force

Polish 303 Fighter Squadron in the sky, 1942

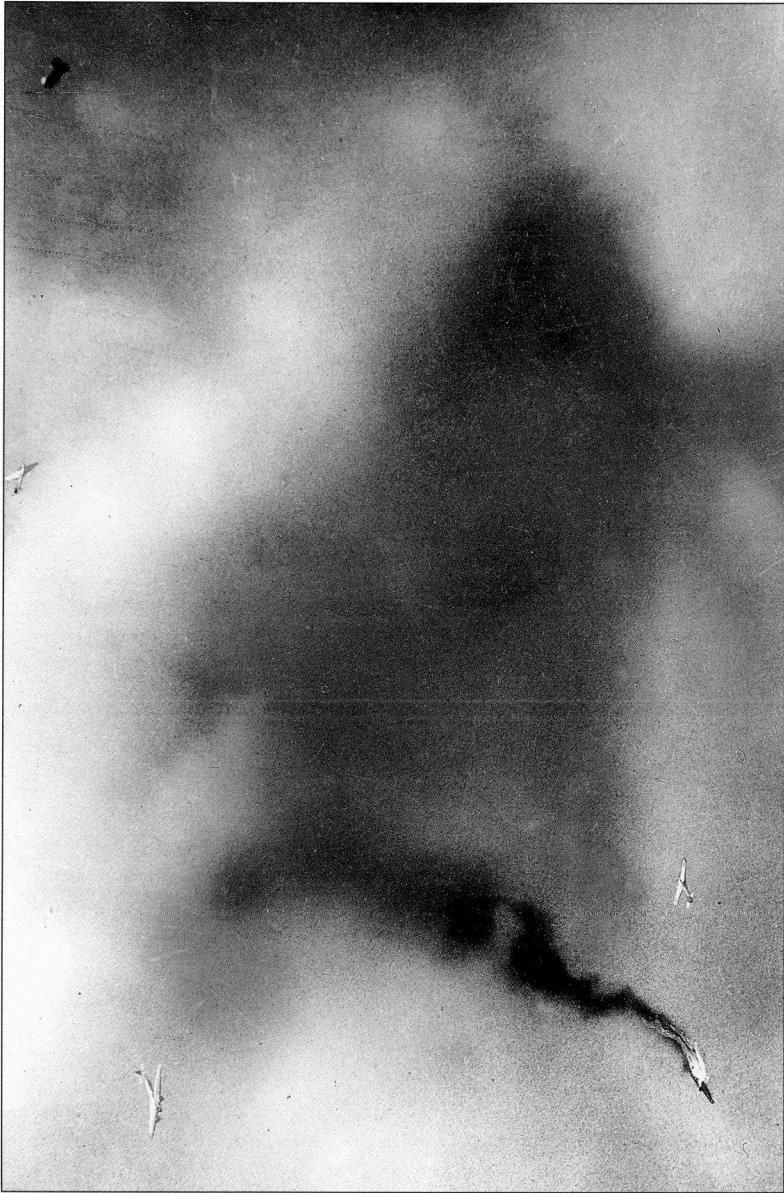

A German plane crashing (note barrage balloon in right top corner)

*A German JU 88 shot down by the Poles, four of the crew
were taken prisoners*

*Sir Archibald Sinclair, Secretary of State for Air visiting
the Polish airmen*

ORP WILK arriving at a British port, September 1939

ORP WICHER, sunk 3.9.1939 in the Baltic, after engagement with the German Navy

ORP KUJAWIAK and KRAKOWIAK docked in Plymouth

ORP BŁYSKAWICA escorting SS Clan Menzies in 1939

Ships of the Polish Merchant Navy in a convoy from Swansea on the eve of the D-Day

ORP PIORUN with torpedoes stacked on her deck

ORP BŁYSKAWICA sustained damage after an air raid 28.4.1942

ORP KRAKOWIAK patrolling off the Lofoten Islands (Norway)

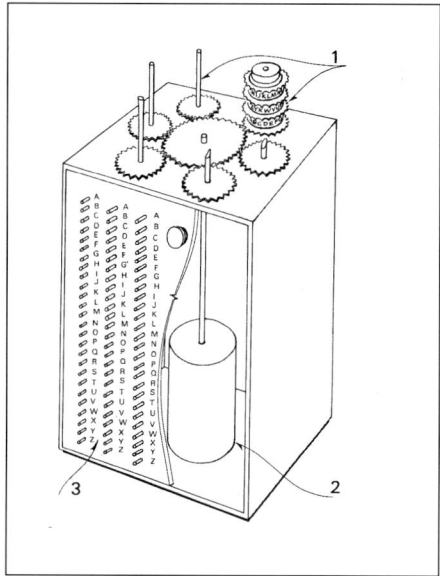

A sketch of the Polish 'bomba' constructed with an aggregate of 6 Enigma rotors

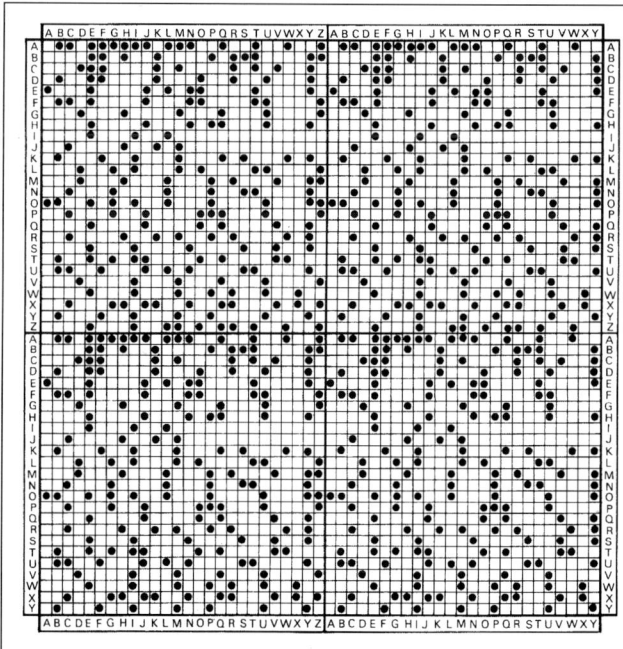

One of Zygalski's perforated sheets, which speeded up the reading of the Enigma machine at its earlier stage

Photographs

'Pipsztok' Radio Transmitter-Receiver constructed by Tadeusz Heftman

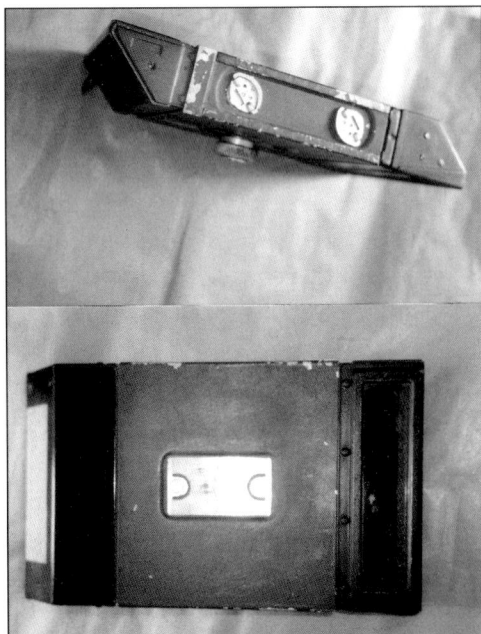

Antoni Gundlach's Directional Periscope, otherwise known as Vickers' Periscope (front and side view).

Thus, in the closing stages of the war, in spite of a vicious circle of proposal and counter-proposal, like a Greek tragedy the Polish politics moved towards the inevitable. While accepting that it was his duty to restore a strong, independent and democratic Poland, Churchill felt that it would have to be politically and territorially acceptable to the Soviet Union and this was the line he pursued in both Teheran and Yalta. He hoped that Stalin, for whom he felt some respect and even sympathy, would relent and allow the Polish Government and Armed Forces to return home. Churchill tried to persuade the Poles that the Russians would in fact keep their pledges to them In reality the fate of Poland and the rest of Eastern Europe were sealed not so much in Yalta as in Teheran in 1943 when the Big Three decided that the main Anglo-American invasion of Europe would take place in northern France. This meant in practice that the Red Army would be the first to enter Poland and that the Polish Home Army could therefore be ultimately successful against the Germans only in co-operation with it. Today we know that – as recently available documents testify – far from envisaging the possibility of such co-operation, Stalin was determined to destroy the Home Army as an obstacle to the establishment of pro-Soviet Polish Government in Warsaw.

Churchill's idea that Stalin would be prepared to deal with an independent, non-Communist Poland, provided that the latter would accept Russian territorial demands, was unrealistic. His attitude to Russia was not yet fully crystallized. In fact, there were occasions when he seemed to be well aware that, with the Red Army in full control over most of Eastern Europe, Great Britain would not be able to discharge her obligations to Poland. On 13 November 1944 the British Prime Minister told General de Gaulle that :

"At present Russia is a great beast which has been starved for a long time. It is not possible to stop her eating, especially since she now lies in the middle of the herd of her victims. The

*question is whether she can be kept from devouring all of them. I
am trying to restrain Stalin who, if he has an enormous appetite,
also has a great deal of good sense. And after the meal comes
the digestion period. When it is time to digest, the surfeited
Russians will have their difficult moments. Then perhaps Saint
Nicholas can bring back to life the poor children the ogre has
put into the salting tub."*

At Yalta Conference, in February 1945, Roosevelt and
Churchill agreed in effect to let Stalin do what he liked with
Poland. Gen. Tadeusz Bór-Komorowski of the Polish Army in
the year 1944-1948 described the Yalta agreement as:
*" Our most painful blow, not from the enemy but from those we
considered our faithful friends. It was entirely incomprehensible
to us why the Allies were giving up to the slavery and partition
their most faithful and oldest ally of the war. It was clear to us
that Yalta was tantamount to blotting out our country's
independence. This blow, so heavy and unexpected shook us to
the core".*

On 5 July 1945, almost six years after the war had
started in defense of Poland's independence, the Allied Powers
withdrew   diplomatic   recognition   from   the   Polish   legal
Government in London. Consequently, the Polish Government
decided that it would relinquish its power and authority only
into the hands of *"a Government which had been formed on the
free Polish soil, according to the existing laws in force in
Poland, one which reflects the freely expressed will of the
people."* Regretfully, the nation had to wait for it for almost half
a century.

During the Second World War our Western Allies –
Great Britain and United States of America were faced with an
insoluble moral, political and military dilemma.   To defeat
Germany, they had to maintain the alliance with Stalin and the
Soviet Union. To maintain the alliance with Moscow they felt
that they had to sacrifice Poland.

It is one of the greatest ironies of the 20th century that the Poles who contributed so much to the allied victory over the Third Reich were made to pay for it by their own friends and allies, at the moment of its very achievement with their own freedom.   And yet through out the entire war we fought in accordance with our centuries old national precept *"For your freedom and ours"* - *"Za waszą i naszą wolność"*.

Role of the Polish Navy in Defence of the British Isles 1939-1945

Teresa Skinder Suchcitz.

> "In Conrad's day the Polish Flag might be looked for in vain in all the Seven Seas. How different it is today. When Poland was wantonly attacked by Germany she had a small but highly efficient modern Navy. In view of its small size, the number of operations in which the Polish Navy has taken part is almost incredible, especially bearing in mind that some of them are continuous. Among these operations are Narvik, Dunkirk, Lofoten Islands, convoy escorting, attacks on shipping and patrols, notably in the Channel and Mediterranean. In May 1941 the Polish destroyer was dauntlessly attacking Bismarck in spite of the great disparity of the two ships in size and armament."

(First Sea Lord of Admiralty A. V. Alexander, 10.2.1944)

ON 1 SEPTEMBER 1939, three Polish destroyers, two large, heavily armed, newly built in Britain ORP[1] 'Błyskawica' (Lightening) and 'Grom'(Thunderclap) and the older 'Burza' (Tempest) entered the port of Leith in Scotland in accordance with an agreement between the Polish and British governments about the use of British ports by units of the Polish Navy in the event of a war with Germany. These units were to be placed under the operational command of the British Admiralty. By the second week of October two submarines, ORP 'Wilk' (Wolf) and 'Orzeł'(Eagle) had joined the destroyers.

This tiny force seemed unlikely to be able to play any significant role in the coming conflict. Yet, from this very

---

[1] Okręt Rzeczypospolitej Polskiej – (Ship of the Republic of Poland)

modest beginning, during the course of the next 6 years, Poland's navy under British operational command expanded to encompass: 9 destroyers, 5 submarines, 2 cruisers, some 10 MGBs and MTBs (Motor Gun and Torpedo Boats) and at times a number of various auxiliary craft. Once the high level of seamanship of the Polish sailors and the competence of the officers had been ascertained by the Admiralty, it was all too pleased to take advantage of this source of trained personnel to man a succession of HMS ships lent to the Polish Navy. In the course of the war, this confidence in the skills of the Polish officers was demonstrated by entrusting them with the position of Senior Officer in command of some of the convoys. Thus the British fleet was augmented by an ally, all too keen to continue fighting for his country at the side of the Royal Navy. On first meeting and inspecting the Polish ships September 1939, Adm. Sir Martin Dunbar-Nasmith C-in-C Western Approaches, wrote in to Cmdr Stankiewicz the senior officer of the flotilla:

'I should like to express my admiration for the splendid spirit of your officers and ships' companies and their evident efficiency[2]. These were the first of many words of praise directed to the Polish authorities throughout the war. In 1947 Adm. Dunbar-Nasmith became the Chairman of the Honorary Committee of the Polish Naval Association. At the end of the war, in a letter to the Head of the Polish Navy, Adm. J. Świrski, The First Lord of the Admiralty expressed the appreciation of the Royal Navy towards their comrades in arms:

---

[2] Instytut Polski i Muzeum gen. Sikorskiego, (Polish Institute and Gen. Sikorski Museum), later as IPMS, MAR. A.V. 16 /1

"I know how much all ranks of the Royal Navy have admired the prowess of the Polish sailors and how glad they are to have had them as comrades in the hard fight against tyranny " [3]

Although the first months of conflict were called the 'phony war', this did not apply to the war at sea which, from its very beginning, was fought with relentless savagery. The U-boat campaign of the First World War had proved so successful, that it had nearly brought Britain to its knees. Lord Jellicoe, the First Sea Lord, told the Cabinet in 1917: *"It is impossible for us to go on with the war if losses like this continue"* [4]. So from the very first days of World War II Germany renewed this successful strategy with a savage onslaught by the U-boats. Their first victim was the liner 'Athenia' outward bound, which was torpedoed on 3 September off the coast of Ireland by the U-30 with the loss of 112 lives. In the beginning, these craft prowled mainly around the coasts of the British Isles looking for easy targets - and there were plenty. Few then operated in the wide waters of the Atlantic – but that was soon to come. The Polish destroyer flotilla sent to its new base in Plymouth via the North of Scotland, attacked on 7 September a U-boat patrolling along the Outer Hebrides and, although a 'kill' did not crown the attack, the Naval authorities acknowledged that the U-boat had been severely damaged.[5]

At first the Polish destroyers had several serious disadvantages when operating from British ports: their construction and capabilities were geared mainly to action in the Baltic and the North Sea, therefore their range was not adapted

---

[3] Quoted by T. Kondracki in *Stowarzyszenie Marynarki Wojennej 1945-1992* (*Polish Naval Association 1945-1992*) Muzeum Marynarki Wojennej (Polish Navy Museum) Gdynia 2003 p.19.

[4] Quoted by Correlli Barnett *Engage the Enemy More Closely* Hodder & Stoughton 1991, p.266.

[5] IPMS, MAR. A.V. 16/1

to the long haul patrols and convoys across the Atlantic. Secondly, their center of gravity - was calculated according to the short, high wave pattern of the Baltic, and not to the huge, long rolling and twisting waves of an Atlantic storm. This rendered then susceptible to serious damage and even to swamping. The first Polish casualty in Britain was caused by this very defect, when a sailor was swept overboard in a moderate sea in the English Channel. Both ORP 'Błyskawica' and 'Grom' underwent modifications to remedy this defect. The Polish vessels were also not equipped with sonar or radar apparatus. Although Poland had shared the secrets of the 'Enigma' with its British and French allies in July 1939, the British did not reciprocate with the apparatus vital in the war at sea. This made detection and fighting U-boats difficult and not as effective as it could have been. Only gradually were Polish ships equipped with asdic and radar.

From October 1939 to March 1940 the three destroyers were based in Harwich and formed part of the Harwich flotilla, an escort group for east and south coast convoys. In those days coal from the north-east coalfields came to London and the South by sea, the railway system was unable to cope with the volume of this traffic. The reciprocal convoys North carried food, and other essential supplies from the port of London and other south coast ports. The safety of these convoys was therefore vital to the war economy. Escorting them was a dangerous, but monotonous task, which combined a maximum of danger with the maximum of discomfort and boredom. The enemy, realising the importance of this traffic, did his utmost to disrupt it. The coastal waters were regularly mined with a variety of differently activated mines and E-boats waited at convenient spots to carry out torpedo attacks. The whole route was strewn with wrecks from unfortunate victims, causing navigational hazards and their shadows provided a convenient spot in which to hide, whilst waiting for the next convoy. The Luftwaffe by day provided an added danger.

Before the outbreak of the war, few people realised the destructive power of air attacks. During the Anglo-Polish Staff talks of May 1939, Capt. Sir Bernard Rawlings, the representative of the Admiralty, averred that: *'The Luftwaffe could only be of nuisance value to warships (in a degree not yet assessed*[6]. How wrong was he! The devastating attacks on HM ships in Norway, during Operation Dynamo, the evacuation of Crete, the Arctic Convoys and on so many other occasions demonstrated the destructive power of air attacks. Already on the 7 November 1939, a lone Heinkel 115 was nearly successful with a torpedo attack on 'Błyskawica' – the first such attack of the war.

During the first months of the war, patrols in the English Channel and near the coast of Belgium and Holland were routine, so was the stopping and checking of neutral shipping, as was done by the 'Błyskawica' with the Latvian s/s 'Rasma' which was escorted to an English port. One of Britain's primary aims was to establish a sea blockade of Germany, cutting her off from all imports arriving by sea. Whenever the opportunity occurred, U-boats were attacked, British mine laying operations were protected, and convoys escorted. It is during this time that the 'Błyskawica' acquired its nickname the 'Biskwitz' as its Polish name caused numerous problems to the British sailors!

The German invasion of Denmark, Norway, and then Holland, Belgium and France brought a change in the tempo of the war. It was the Polish submarine 'Orzeł' which sounded the alarm when she stopped and then torpedoed the German vessel 'Rio de Janeiro' carrying troops for the invasion of Norway. The debacle in Norway followed, with the loss of several valuable units of the Royal Navy, including the aircraft carrier HMS 'Glorious'. Among the casualties were also, the destroyer

---

[6] IPMS, *Bellona* III-IV London 1958, Minutes of the Anglo-Polish Staff meeting, May 1939.

'Grom' and the modern liner s/s 'Chrobry' (King of Poland in the Middle Ages), acting as a troopship both were bombed and sunk with considerable loss of life. ORP 'Orzeł' too, was lost at this time. This amounted to 2/5ths of the Polish ships then serving under British command.

Worse was to follow the blitzkrieg and the fall of France, which stranded the British Expeditionary Force – troops vital to the coming defense of the British Isles. The famous evacuation from Dunkirk, which saved some 340.000 men, if not their equipment, was a magnificent feat performed by the Royal Navy. By the end of May 1940, with the British and French forces in full retreat from Flanders and Northern France towards the Channel ports, the Royal Navy began evacuating troops from Calais and then from Dunkirk. Both remaining Polish destroyers took part in this action.

The 'Burza' in company with two destroyers from the Harwich fleet, received orders to patrol along the French coast and shell the advancing German columns. Shortly afterwards some 30 bombers attacked the destroyers. 'Burza' had one definite and one probable kill, but was herself hit. It was only through the strenuous efforts of the engine room crew that a slow stern first withdrawal to Dover was possible. HMS 'Vimera' was severely crippled, but HMS 'Wessex' was sunk in this action[7].

During the evacuation the role assigned to the 'Błyskawica' was to patrol the Channel and ensure, as far as it was possible, the safety of the evacuation fleet. She took on tow the badly damaged HMS 'Greyhound' overloaded with soldiers and wounded and brought them safely to Dover. She also rescued 15 persons from the torpedoed French destroyer 'Sirocco'[8].

---

[7] IPMS, MAR. A.V. 17/1. Also S. Piaskowski *Kroniki Marynarki Wojennej* (*Annals of the Polish Navy*) vol. 2, Sigma Press New York, 1987 p. 131.
[8] IPMS, MAR. A.V. 16/2

With the fall of France and her long Atlantic seacoast in German hands, the invasion of Britain seemed imminent. Every available craft was pressed into service, and so a group of 12 Dutch and French trawlers was handed over by the Admiralty to the Polish Navy, to act as patrol boats in the Channel, with their main task to watch out for the first signs of the invasion fleet. Two submarine chasers: 'Chasseurs' 11 and 15, two patrol boats, the 'Medoc' and the 'Pomerol', and the destroyer 'Ouragan' were also handed over to the Polish Navy and served under two flags: Polish and French. The smaller craft were returned to the Admiralty by the end of October 1940, their state of repair being such, that frequent stays in the dockyard became a necessity. For a time the 'Medoc' served with a mixed crew with Cmdr Stankiewicz as CO. It was the only ship in the war to raise three flags at once: Polish, British and French. Unfortunately it was sunk with a loss of lives including her captain. 1940 saw the increase of the Polish naval forces by two fully operational destroyers: HMS 'Garland', which kept her name at the request of the Royal Navy, as there had been an HMS 'Garland' in service since 1242. HMS 'Nerissa', became ORP 'Piorun' (Thunderbolt). It was 'Piorun's' leading seaman E. Dolecki, (after the war he served in the Royal Navy), who first sighted the 'Bismarck', which had disappeared into the darkness of the night and the pursuing Home Fleet had temporarily lost contact. Cmdr Pławski, 'Piorun's' captain, gave orders to open fire on the German battleship and transmitted her exact position to the pursuing force[9].

1941-42 saw further increases in the size of the Polish Navy: the submarine fleet was augmented by three new craft, the ex US 'Jastrząb' (Hawk), sunk in the North Sea by friendly fire, and the new British built ORP 'Sokół' (Falcon) and 'Dzik' (Wild Hog), the 'Terrible Twins' which earned much glory in

---

[9]   IPMS, MAR. A.V. 19/5; *Kroniki* vol 2. p. 175-176. Also Capt. E. Pławski *Fala za Falą (Wave after Wave)*, Finna Press, Gdańsk, 2003, p. 364 – 394.

their campaigns in the Mediterranean. By April 1941 the 'Huragan'(Hurricane), due to her frequent breakdowns, had become a liability and was handed back to the French. Its crew formed the basis for manning two Hunt class destroyers ORP 'Krakowiak' (folk dance from Kraków region) and 'Kujawiak' (folk dance from Kujawy region). In April 1942 they were joined by a third, ORP 'Ślązak' (Silesian) (ex HMS Bedale).

Until the danger of a German invasion faded in 1941, all Polish ships, together with their British counterparts fulfilled a vital role: no invasion could take place as long as the Germans did not gain the mastery of the air, and the Royal Navy remained undefeated. It was a time of ceaseless patrols making sure that the sea routes around British coasts remained open, that no German convoys or even individual vessels could sail unchallenged in the Channel and also a continued relentless fight with the Luftwaffe out to attack all shipping and ports. A typical incident in this kind of warfare was the defence in March 1942 of convoy PW 125 sailing from Falmouth to Milford Haven. The first JU-88 was sighted near Land's End and the first attack was driven off by ORP 'Kujawiak's' Oerlikon guns, later on her gunners successfully shot down one enemy bomber. The attacks continued at five-minute intervals with all escort ships providing a sustained defence, which enabled all ships to reach their destination[10]. In this kind of work the Polish motor gun and torpedo boats, together with the three Hunt destroyers played an important role. The MGBs S2 and S3 were handed over to the Poles in exchange for one of the two artillery torpedo boats being built for them before 1939 by S.J. White. Ultimately 10 such craft would be in service under the Polish flag.

MGB S2's best known action took place in June 1942 against a group of six German torpedo boats in the Channel.

---

[10] IPMS, MAR. A.V.21/2 and *Kroniki* vol. 3 p. 19-20.

The S2 and S3 were sent out on patrol when the S3 developed an engine breakdown and had to return to base. The CO of S2, in spite of a radioed message to return to base as well, with a truly 'Nelsonian' touch pretended not to understand the order and continued with the patrol. A group of six German torpedo boats was sighted; the S2 took up her position between them and the French coast and attacked casting the enemy into utter confusion. During this action two enemy boats were damaged, and with the arrival of help, the Germans were forced to withdraw [11]. It was also a group of destroyers and MTBs, among them the Polish S2 and S3, which was sent to attack the German battleships 'Scharnhorst' and "Gneisenau" making a dash from Brest to German ports. The heavy units of the Home Fleet were nowhere near to carry out this task.

Another incident in this kind of warfare was the patrol carried out by ORP 'Kujawiak' in company with HMS 'Atherstone', who were tasked with finding and destroying a small German convoy hugging the coast of France in the direction of Cherbourg. On reaching their sector near the island of Alderney, two merchantmen were sighted. Atherstone opened fire on the leading ship, while 'Kujawiak' took on the second one. After the third salvo, the lookout noticed the stern and the bow sinking under the waves. A third merchantman came into view and after accurate artillery fire it too sunk. Both ships were ordered back to harbour [12]. Several weeks later, ORP 'Krakowiak' was involved in a similar action off Guernsey. Such operations were the normal bread and butter of service in the Channel in which the Hunt destroyers and the motor gunboats took part. If attack is the best method of defence, there was no lack of such incidents. There was in November 1940 the shelling by HMS 'Revenge' of Cherbourg used as a naval base

---

[11] *Kroniki* vol.3. p.46. Jerzy Pertek *Wielkie Dni Małej Floty, (Great Days of the Small Fleet)*, Wydawnictwo Poznańskie, 1990 p.341-2

[12] IPMS, MAR. A.V. and *Kroniki* vol.3 p.13.

by the Germans, the Polish S2 and S3 formed part of the escort. Another was the raid on Dieppe (August 1942) in which ORP 'Ślązak' took part shooting down 4 enemy planes and rescuing 15 men from the sea.

While in harbour, all ships formed a vital part of the anti-aircraft defence. One of the main German war aims was to destroy the dockyards and port facilities, thus depriving the Royal Navy of its operational bases. There are many accounts of the Polish ships engaged in such operations. In March 1941 during a particularly heavy air raid on Greenock, ORP 'Piorun', which had just returned from convoy duty, helped to provide the anti-aircraft defence, ships were hit, among them 'Piorun' herself, and its crew was involved in putting out not only its own fires, but those on several other ships, among them on HMS 'Duke of York', which was nearing completion in the dockyard. While the MGB S2 shot down a Heinkel 111 during one of the many air raids on Portsmouth.

The best known of these air defences was the one in which ORP 'Błyskawica' and the Polish merchant ship, s/s 'Kmicic' (a fictitious hero) just arrived with a cargo, took part in April–May 1942. The destroyer was then undergoing thoroughgoing repairs and rearmament in the dockyards of S.J. White her builders, in Cowes. Cowes its port and the town itself were under ceaseless air attacks and on this occasion the guns of the destroyer played an important role in their defence. On the night of 5-6 May there was a series of particularly bad air raids lasting through the night, with flare bombs illuminating the whole dockyard area, followed by a rain of incendiary ones, which started a series of serious fires. The machine-guns of the 'Kmicic' concentrated on shooting down the parachute flares, and its Oerlikon and six-pounder added to the barrage. The guns of the 'Błyskawica' providing the main barrage forced the aircraft to fly at a higher altitude; a smoke screen was laid on, which obscured some of the targets. A group of 20 sailors was sent to help the fire fighters in the dockyard area, another 30 sailors were sent to help put out the fires in the aircraft factory of Sanders Roe. Later on the ship's doctor with a nursing unit was sent to West Cowes. Another group was sent to deal with a fuel fire in the dockyard area. Great damage was caused that night, but the directors of the shipyards, the police chief and indeed the citizens of Cowes firmly believed that it was thanks to the barrage provided by the Polish destroyer that there was not a greater loss of life and property. There were deputations to thank the crew for their help and the CO was presented with a historic Polish medal dating back to the year 1788. With the passing of the years Cowes has not forgotten their Polish defenders, not only is there a commemorative plaque in the shipyard, and a ceremony of remembrance is held each year [13].

So far only the immediate defence of the British Isles has been discussed. Yet we must remember, that it would have been in vein, were it not for the steady supply of food – British agriculture being unable to produce enough to feed the population - fuel, and other raw materials vital to the war production, as well as armaments, which arrived in British ports from the USA and Commonwealth countries. Without them Britain would not have been able to continue to fight the war. In 1941 British imports of dry cargo were running at 73% of estimated tonnage requirements, while imports of oil were running at 10% below.[14] The following eighteen months were to prove just as disastrous. The defence of the convoys carrying these precious supplies was therefore of primary importance for Britain's very survival and her fighting capability.

All the Polish destroyers, but especially 'Błyskawica', 'Burza', 'Piorun', 'Garland' and then ORP 'Orkan' (Cyclone) took part in the Battle of the Atlantic, this vital struggle to take

---

[13] IPMS, MAR. A.V. 16/5 and IPMS, A.42.
[14] Correlli Barnett *Engage the Enemy More Closely* p. 266.

the convoys through and to keep the shipping lanes across the Atlantic open. Each had its successes and moments of glory. ORP 'Burza's' came in its defence of convoy ON 166 in February 1943. The convoy was attacked in mid Atlantic by a wolf pack and 'Burza' was despatched to strengthen the defence. Catching up with the convoy, she first torpedoed an abandoned Norwegian freighter, which could cause navigational hazards to future convoys. Then, she got a strong echo on her asdic, indicating one of the attacking U-boats. A sustained depth charge attack forced the German to surface and to send SOS signals. It was immediately rammed by the corvette USS 'Campbell'. 'Burza' sent a boat to collect the crew from the sinking U-boat. She also took on board most of the American sailors, as their craft had been seriously damaged, she then sailed for Newfoundland. The CO of the 'Campbell' described the Polish destroyer as *"the fightingest ship we have ever seen"*[15].

There were tragedies as well. ORP 'Orkan', (ex HMS 'Myrmidon'), incorporated into the Polish Navy in November 1942, was sunk in October 1943 by a German torpedo when escorting convoy SC143, with the loss of 178 of its crew, including her captain, Cmdr Hryniewiecki[16]. The first Polish cruiser ORP 'Dragon' (she kept her British name), which after a lengthy refit came into service in time for Operation Neptune, as the naval part of the invasion of Normandy was called, when it was torpedoed and badly damaged. She was then sunk as a part of the Mulberry harbour. The replacement cruiser ORP 'Conrad' (ex HMS 'Danae'), came into service right at the end of the war. If the Atlantic convoys formed part of the long-range defence of the British Isles, then the Arctic convoys to Archangel and

---

[15] IPMS, MAR. A.V. 17/12. *Kroniki Marynarki Wojennej (Annals..)*vol. 3 p. 73.
[16] Tadeusz Kondracki *Niszczyciel Orkan 1942-1945, (Destroyer Orkan 1942-1945,* Lampart, Fenix Editions 1994.

Murmansk were part of the indirect defence. They were essential in supplying the necessary war materials to the Soviet Union, without which, it would have been unable to carry on fighting. These supplies provided a breathing space to the beleaguered Russians, allowing home industries to develop and take over the provision of the essential armaments. To keep the Soviet Union in the war was seen by the Western leaders as a sine qua non of winning the struggle against Hitler's Germany. So despite very heavy losses, a steady stream of convoys continued to make the hazardous journey beyond the Arctic Circle. Polish warships ORP 'Piorun', 'Garland' and 'Orkan' took part in them. Polish sailors were uneasy about these operations. The Soviet Union had treacherously invaded their country in September 1939. Many of them had been deported to the slave camps in Siberia; many of their families had also been uprooted and sent beyond the Urals. Yet, as loyal allies under the orders of the Admiralty, they performed their duty. ORP 'Garland' was part of the escort of the summer convoy PQ 16, which with a reduced escort, came under a sustained attack from both the Luftwaffe and the U-boats. 'Garland' fought a long duel with the German bombers in the defence of her charges. The casualty count on the destroyer was so heavy, that she received permission to make a quick lone passage to Murmansk to deliver the wounded to hospital[17]. She suffered 25 crewmen killed and had 43 wounded on board. Before the convoy reached its destination out of 36 merchantmen seven had been lost carrying 150 tanks, 77 aircraft, and 770 motor vehicles.[18]

---

[17] IPMS, MAR. A.V. 20/3. Also *Kroniki (Annals..)* vol 3 p. 133 - 136 and Bohdan Pawłowicz, *ORP Garland in convoy to Russia*, Surrey Press 1943.
[18] IPMS, MAR. AV. 20/3. Also *Kroniki Marynarki Wojennej, (Annals..)* vol. 3 p.33-36; Bohdan Pawłowicz *Krew na Oceanie* (*Blood on the Ocean*), Rytm, Warszawa 1991; Z. Damski *ORP Garland*, Bellona, Warszawa, p. 106-127

One cannot omit the contribution made by the Polish Merchant Fleet to the defence of Britain. At the outbreak of the war, 42 ships of over 250 BRT flew the Polish flag and during its course 14 others were either taken on loan or bought outright. Four large, new liners, the pride of the Polish fleet, were converted into troopships. Such was the demand for merchant ships, as the tempo of sinking by enemy action mounted, that even veterans like the liner s/s 'Kościuszko' (veteran of the American wars and hero of the Polish national rising of 1794), which at the beginning of the war had served as a base ship for the Polish Navy, were pressed into active service.

All these vessels, serving in all the areas of conflict, played a valuable role in keeping Britain supplied with indispensable troops and raw materials and were of special value in the Atlantic convoys. As with the warships there were sad losses: The first Polish ship to be lost outside the Baltic was m/s 'Piłsudski" (a true hero of the 1920 Polish War of Independence), in November 1939 off the coast of Northumberland, then s/s 'Chrobry' (King of Poland in the Middle Ages), was sunk during the Norwegian campaign. In all 14 ships totaling 63.463 BRT were lost due to enemy action.[19]

When the two veterans of the Polish Navy, the destroyer 'Burza' and the submarine 'Wilk' became past their best fighting capabilities, they continued to provide a vital service as training ships, using their experience and skills to pass them on to new generations of British and Polish sailors.

In these several ways the Polish Navy made a not unimportant contribution to the defence of Great Britain. There remains of course the various technical advances, adaptations and inventions, which in the course of the war years added to the technical developments, which made the war at sea so much more effective. First and foremost was the breaking of the most

---

[19] Jerzy Pertek *Druga Mała Flota, (The Second Small Fleet)*, re. Polish Merchant Navy at war, Poznań 1958, p. 276-280.

secret German coding system and then the building a working model of the Enigma machine itself. This is not the place to discuss this achievement, except to say, that without this initial breakthrough and the generous action of the pre-war Polish government in passing this momentous information together with a working model of the machine to Poland's allies, who knows how the Battle of the Atlantic would have fared? As it was, it was touch and go at times, whether Britain could win it. To mention but one improvement developed by Sub-Lieutenant Jan Buchowski to the stereoscopic range finder, which enabled to determine very accurately the moment when shells of an anti- aircraft gun passed near its target. After lengthy correspondence with the Admiralty and Ministry of Supply and various experiments, this was accepted as facilitating accurate firing and thus important in air defence [20]

Under British operational command during six years of the war at sea, the achievements of The Polish Navy can be thus summarised: Altogether the ships sailed 1213 thousand miles, jointly they escorted 787 convoys, took part in 1162 patrols and naval actions; they sank 7 enemy naval surface craft, 41 merchant ships and 3 U-boats; 20 aircraft were shot down and they had 10 probable kills. Own losses amounted to 450 men killed and 7 naval craft sunk, (the submarine 'Orzeł' with its entire crew) as well as two large, modern liners converted to troopships[21]. To sum up: one can divide the Polish naval contribution into several sections:

Firstly, the defence of the home waters, i.e. coastal convoys, patrols in the Bristol and English Channels right up to the coasts of France, Belgium and Holland and in the North Sea.

---

[20] The National Archive (TNA, formerly PRO) ADM 1/10285.
[21] *Polska Marynarka Wojenna 1939 – 1945, (Polish Navy 1939-1945),* vol.1. choice of documents edited by Z. Wojciechowski, Polish Navy Museum, Gdynia, 1999, p.14.

It was a struggle to keep the coastal convoys safe, to prevent the activities of the E-Boats and to establish a blockade of Germany by stopping her sea trade.

Secondly, the provision of anti-aircraft defence of British ports and dockyard installations. This was very important in the context of ceaseless German bombing raids whose aims was to cripple the Royal Navy and by depriving her of vital bases and so making continued operations at sea impossible.

Thirdly, the long-range defence through the protection of convoys bringing vital supplies, which enabled Britain to continue fighting the war and the indirect defence through the Arctic convoys, which kept the Soviet Union in the war.

Fourthly, the technical improvements starting with Enigma, through to all the other inventions, which do not have an equivalent glamour as the actions at sea, and are not so widely described in the annals of the Polish Navy.

Finally, by providing a core of well trained officers, NCOs and a growing number of sailors, which made it possible for the Admiralty to increase the number of fighting ships under its command. We must also add the value of an experienced submarine and destroyer for the purposes of training officers and crews engaged in the actual fighting. Thus the small Polish Navy under British operational Command made a valuable contribution to the fighting capability of the Royal Navy and the defence of the British Isles.

"The Best All-Round Players in the Game"

Michael Smith

IT FALLS TO ME HERE to offer a British perspective on the Polish contribution to intelligence in the Second World War. As a British historian, who has written extensively about Bletchley Park, I must say I feel as if I have walked, rather like Daniel, into the Lion's Den. I will say at the outset, and in my own defence, that I have always taken great care in my own books to point out that without the Poles, the British code breakers would never have got started until at the very earliest, the Norwegian campaign in April 1940, when a machine and a set of rotors were captured.[22]

The first British encounter with the Enigma cipher machine occurred in 1921 when they were offered an early pre-production model with a view to using it for their own communications. There appears to have been no take-up of this but in 1926, Hugh Foss, a code breaker in the Government Code and Cipher School, then based not at Bletchley Park, but at Broadway, above the St James's underground station, was asked to examine the small commercial machine.[23] For those of you unfamiliar with Enigma machine, it looked essentially like a small typewriter. On most models, there was a standard continental QWERTZU keyboard, as opposed to the British QWERTY, and above that a lamp board with a series of lights one for each letter of the alphabet. Inside the machine were a series of

---

[22] Hugh Foss, *Reminiscences on Enigma,* Michael Smith & Ralph Erskine, *Action This Day,* Bantam Press 2001.
[23] ibidem

three, or sometimes later in the war four, rotors, which were the main elements of the decipherment system. The operator typed in the letters of the plain text message. The action of depressing the key sent an electrical impulse through the machine and the enciphered letters lit up on the lamp board. Breaking the cipher rested on the cryptanalyst's ability to determine the internal wiring of the machine and the way in which it was changed every time the operator pressed a key. The commercial machine was an infinitely inferior machine to the 'steckered' machine that was to be used later by the German armed forces. Foss found it relatively easy to break and the British decided not to take up the offer.[24]

Not so the German armed forces that did of course decide to use the machine. The British at this point seemed to have little interest in breaking the German codes and ciphers. The Germans had been denuded of any power by Versailles. The British code breakers were concerned with the rise in naval power of the United States and Japan. It is with hindsight perhaps amusing to note that the section concerned with breaking the US codes was the largest within the British code breaking organisation in the 1920s, although this seems likely to have had as much to do with the rise of US commercial power as the strength of its navy. Britain was already being ousted as a global superpower by the lost colonies in America. The other main focus, for very understandable reasons, was on the Soviet Union. The 1920s and the 1930s was the period of the first cold war and British intercept operations in the Middle East, the Indian sub-continent and even here in London were heavily focused on the Bolsheviks.[25]

[24] The National Archives (TNA), HW3/1; HW3/3; HW3/16, recollections of William 'Nobby' Clarke
[25] Michael Smith, *Station X, Decoding Nazi Secrets,* USA 1998.

Why did the British not bother with the German codes and ciphers until it was almost too late? Josh Cooper, the head of the Air Section at Bletchley Park, who appears in the Report of the Anglo-Polish Historical Committee as a firm advocate of the crucial role the Poles were to play, said that the British decided early on that the German codes and ciphers would be unbreakable. 'Considering what Room 40 had achieved in 1914-18, it seems extraordinary that anyone could believe this. But it was generally assumed that no civilised nation that had once been through the traumatic experience of having its ciphers read would ever allow it to happen again and that, after the wide publicity given to Room 40's result, it would be a waste of time working on German high-grade systems.[26]

Fortunately, the Poles and the French, each immediately threatened by the resurgence of the German military in the early 1930s, took a different view. They worked together but in code breaking terms the Poles were of course the masters. The Polish Cipher Bureau (Biuro Szyfrów – BS) had understandably concentrated on German codes and ciphers during the 1920s, breaking them without major problems until 1926, when the German navy adopted two simple versions of Enigma. When the German Army also adopted the Enigma machine in 1929, the bureau realised that it had long-term problems. Breaking the new machine ciphers would require the skill of trained mathematicians. The bureau recruited a number of mathematics students and put them through a course in cryptanalysis. Only three completed the course. Their names: Jerzy Różycki, Henryk Zygalski and Marian Rejewski. They began working for BS4, the section dealing with German codes and ciphers, although initially only on a part-time basis.[27] It was at this point, with the British

[26] Władysław Kozaczuk, *Enigma. How the German Machine Cipher as broken and how it was read by the Allies in the World War Two,* Arms & Armour Press 1984.
[27] Ralph Erskine, Breaking Air Force & Army Enigma, in *Action This Day.*

code breakers still showing little interest in Germany, that the German army added a plug board to the machine, transforming it from a relatively easy machine to break, not greatly dissimilar to the commercial machine broken by Foss, into a very much more secure cipher system, greatly increasing the possible decipherment variations. These would eventually reach an astonishing 159 million. At this stage the more experienced Polish code breakers attempted to break the new Enigma machine, without success. It was not until September 1932, two years after its introduction, that it was given to Marian Rejewski, the best of the three young mathematicians to investigate on his own. Within just a few months, in a truly magnificent feat of cryptanalysis that matches anything done before or since, Rejewski had reconstructed the wiring of Enigma's rotors mathematically, using permutation theory.[28]

By January 1933, the Poles were reading Enigma telegrams, but successive changes introduced by the Germans made that process more difficult. As the Polish code breakers overcame each difficulty, so another was added. In 1938, as part of the efforts to overcome new changes designed to make the machine more secure, Rejewski devised a mechanical machine, the *bomba* to exploit the indicating system. Despite the name, this was not the same machine as the Bombes invented much later by the British code breaker Alan Turing, which formed the main basis for the breaking of the Enigma ciphers at Bletchley Park. Both used the principle of linking up series of rotors. But the Polish *bomba* attacked the message key and was therefore vulnerable to a relatively simple change in German procedure. The British bombe used a crib of likely plain text to attack the message itself and was therefore immune to such changes.[29]

---

[28] Donald E. Davies, 'The Bombe, a remarkable logic machine', *Cryptologia*, 23 (1999) 108

[29] Kozaczuk, *Enigma.*.

Another innovation introduced by the Poles, and one that was to prove invaluable to the later British attacks on Enigma, was the invention by Henryk Zygalski of sets of perforated sheets, which were used to break the keys and settings on the machine.

Perhaps the most important of the many changes the Germans made after introducing the plug board was the introduction in December 1938 of two more rotors, allowing the use of any three from a selection of five. Within weeks, Rejewski had reconstructed the wiring of the new rotors. But by now the difficulties had mounted up to the point where the Poles knew they had to seek help and proposed a joint meeting with the French and the British.[30]

The excellent chapter on Cryptographic Cooperation in the report suggests, citing Col Stefan Mayer, the former Polish intelligence chief, that there was some reluctance on the part of the British to attend the initial meeting, to be held in Paris in January 1939.[i] There is no evidence of this in British accounts, rather the reverse, and it may well be that this impression was the result of Gustav Bertrand of the French Deuxième Bureau, who was liaising with both the Poles and the British, playing the two sides off against each other. The British had been cooperating with Bertrand since 1933 on Russian ciphers but it had been a largely one-sided cooperation with the French producing little.[31]

As a result of the rather dubious British belief that Germany was not a significant threat and that at any event its ciphers would be impossible to break, the British had carried out very little work on Enigma during the 1930s. It was not until the

---

[30] Jan S. Ciechanowski & Jacek Tebinka, Cryptographic Co-operation – Enigma, *Intelligence Co-operation Between Poland and Great Britain During World War II, The Report of the Anglo-Polish Historical Committee* Vol. 1, edited by Tessa Stirling, Daria Nałęcz & Tadeusz Dubicki, Valentine Mitchell London 2005.
[31] TNA, HW3/83, J E S Cooper's personal notes on GC&CS 1925-1939.

Spanish Civil War in 1936, that there was any real attempt to break live Enigma traffic. After some initial work by Josh Cooper, Dilly Knox broke an Enigma machine provided by the Germans to the Italians and Spanish in April 1937, using similar principles to those used by Foss when he broke the commercial machine.[32]

The British were confident that they could break the German army Enigma using four streams of text from an Enigma message in both its original and enciphered form provided to them by the French (whether they were obtained from Asche or the Poles is not clear, although the latter seems the most likely). But to break the machine the British needed to work out the way in which the keys were connected to the contacts on the entry plate at the start of the machine's wiring. In the case of the commercial machine these had been wired up in the order they appeared on the keyboard, beginning at the left of the top row with Q connected to A, and then running left to right along the three rows to M at the right-hand side of the bottom row, M being connected to Z. As a result, the British nicknamed this the QWERTZU after the order of letters on the top row of the continental-style keyboard used on the machine. The British had no idea what the QWERTZU was for the machines used by the German armed forces.[33]

The first meeting in Paris produced little. The Poles had been ordered to hold back on any information they had until they were sure that the British or the French had something to contribute. But at a second meeting in the Pyry Forest near Warsaw in July 1939, the Poles revealed their achievements, including the use of the *bomby* and the Zygalski sheets. Dilly Knox was initially furious to discover that the Poles had got there

---

[32] Foss, Reminiscences..
[33] Foss, Reminiscences..; Erskine, Breaking Air Force...; Peter Twinn, The Abwehr Enigma in F H Hinsley & Alan Stripp, Code Breakers, *The Inside Story of Bletchley Park,* OUP, Oxford 1993.

first, which may be the origins of the suggestion in the report, again not substantiated by any of the British accounts, that the British took offence at not having been told earlier.[34] But once Rejewski told him the details of the QWERTZU, Knox was deliriously happy and so impressed by the Polish achievements, that he immediately began lobbying Alistair Denniston, the head of the British code breaking establishment GC&CS to have the Polish code breakers brought to the UK.[35]

At the outbreak of war, the Polish code breakers were evacuated to France working at the French code breaking centre PC Bruno, based in a chateau at Gretz-Armainvillers, 40 miles east of Paris. It was here that, after being supplied with the necessary stock of Zygalski sheets, they made the first break of the war into the Enigma cipher, breaking the 'Green' cipher used to communicate between German army military districts on 17 January 1940. It was shortly afterwards that Bletchley Park made its first break into a Wehrmacht Enigma, also the 'Green' cipher, an accomplishment that was only possible as a result of the information provided by the Poles.[36] The revelation of how to break the Enigma machine were undoubtedly the greatest service provided to the British by the Polish intelligence services. But it was not, as this report makes clear, the only one.

The Polish contribution to the work of the Secret Intelligence Service, now better known as MI6, may not have been quite so crucial as the Polish contribution was for the British code breakers, but it was every bit as productive. MI6 began the war in retreat. Lack of funding during the inter-war years, a foolish decision to combine its heads of station in the European capitals with a fallback network of covert officers, and the swift German advance across Europe, first to the east and

---

[34] TNA, HW25/12, A G Denniston, How news was brought from Warsaw at the end of July 1939.
[35] TNA, HW25/12, Knox to Denniston, July 1939.
[36] Erskine, Breaking Air Force..

then the west, left Britain with very few spies in place. One note of caution here. In recent years, it has begun to emerge, that there were very many more than we have been led to believe, particularly in Germany itself.[37] But it was clear that with the intelligence picture of occupied Europe at worst shattered and at best opaque, any assistance they could get from the intelligence services of those countries now occupied by the Nazis would have improved their knowledge. In the event, the intelligence they received was critical. The three countries whose intelligence services provided the most information at the start of the war were the Poles, the Czechs and the Norwegians. All three provided a brilliant service, but the jewel in the crown was without a shadow of a doubt, the intelligence provided by the Polish II Bureau.

The key to this lay in the fact that Poland still regarded itself as one of the Great Powers and had an intelligence service to match. As the report shows, the Poles had spies quite literally everywhere and could supply intelligence not only from across Europe but on the Soviet Union, the Far East and Latin America. They were in the words of John Colville, Churchill's private secretary, *probably the best of the all round players in the game'.*[38] Picking people out of such a rich tapestry is invidious but perhaps I might be forgiven for selecting two of my personal favourites as two of the most sparkling facets of this jewel in the crown of wartime intelligence.

The first receives only scant mention in the report. Tragically, it seems, little detail has survived in any of the archives. I was however fortunate enough, before he died, to interview one of the MI6 officers involved in the operation,

---

[37] Michael Smith, *The Spying Game: The Sicret History of British Espionage,* Politicos, London 2004; Philip H J Davies, *MI6 and the Machinery of Spying,* Frank Cass, London 2004.
[38] John Colville, *Strange Inheritance,* Michael Russell, Wilton 1983.

which was based in Berne, in Switzerland. It centred on Halina Szymańska, the wife of the former Polish military attaché in Berlin. She and her husband were friends of the head of the Abwehr, Admiral Wilhelm Canaris.

Madame Szymańska turned out to be a very significant contact, the former MI6 officer said. 'Canaris was violently anti-Nazi and was involved in plotting against Hitler. He took a very dim view of what the Nazis were up to and as head of the Abwehr, where he could, he managed to commute death sentences to life sentences where agents were involved, including some British agents. He had a penchant for attractive ladies. He is supposed to have placed four at various posts overseas. Madame Szymańska was the wife of the Polish military attaché in Berlin before the war. They were both very friendly with Canaris. He rescued her after the Russians had captured her husband during the Soviet occupation of Poland. Canaris was able to arrange for her and her children to travel in a sealed railway carriage across Germany from Poland to Switzerland, where he maintained contact with her. Indeed, he himself visited her in Berne a number of times.'

On arrival in Berne, Madame Szymańska had reported her story to the Polish embassy, which passed it on to Polish intelligence officers based in London with the government in exile, the officer said. The head of the Polish II Bureau in London 'brought it to Claude Dansey [the MI6 assistant chief] and said, *"This is a very hot potato. It is the best I can ever give you and it is so secret that I don't trust my own people to handle it, so I am giving it to you,"* he said. Dansey then sent Frederick van den Heuvel out to Switzerland and told him: *"Your number one mission in life is to handle this woman. Everything else is second class."* Canaris talked very freely to Madame Szymańska about German intentions. He was either extremely indiscreet or using her as an intentional conduit to pass information to the allies. Dansey was determined to keep the information totally secure, and at the Berne station only van den Heuvel was briefed on what was going on. Dansey kept the whole of the Swiss station and its activities in his own hands in headquarters. He wouldn't let the files go out. He wouldn't give them the general circulation that they should have. His story was: *"I started the Swiss station. It's my station and I'm running it from here"*.[39]

The product of Source Warlock, as Madame Szymańska was known, began in the spring of 1940 with the news that the main German thrust against France would go through the Ardennes, a claim that was sadly not believed.[40] Later that year, she provided a full rundown of German plans to invade Greece via Bulgaria and Yugoslavia, which would be occupied 'with or without' its government's permission. The former MI6 officer said: 'The most important item Szymańska reported was in January 1941, when she was able to tell us that an irrevocable decision had been made by Hitler, against the advice of his staff, to attack Russia in May of that year. At this time the main German military effort appeared to be preparing the invasion of England in the spring. This valuable nugget of intelligence foretold a relaxation of the pressures on England and a future sharing of the war burden with Russia. Sir Stafford Cripps, our ambassador in Moscow, passed this information - suitably disguised, together with some other, probably Ultra, items on the subject - to the Russians. Unfortunately, Stalin discounted it as misinformation from the British intelligence service.[41]

---

[39] Information provided to the author in confidence. See Robert Cecil, C's War, *Intelligence and National Security*, Vol.1, no. 2 April 1986; ICB Dear (editor), The Oxford Companion to the Second World War, OUP, Oxford 1995; Nigel West, *MI6 ; British Secret Intelligence Service Operations 1909-1945*, Weidenfeld & Nicholson, London 1983.
[40] Józef Garliński, The Swiss Corridor, Dent, London 1981.
[41] Information provided to the author in confidence.

The Joint Intelligence Committee however had no doubt as to the importance of the Szymanska material, describing it as the *'most valuable and amongst the best reports received from any quarter'.* Sir Stewart Menzies, the MI6 wartime Chief, believed to his deathbed that more use might have been made of Szymanska's links to Berlin, telling a colleague that Canaris had made an offer of talks that he had been ready to accept 'but Eden [the British Foreign Secretary] stopped me'. Shortly before he died, Menzies disclosed that he had hoped *'to open discussions with Admiral Canaris on the removal of Hitler as a means of shortening the war and negotiating peace. But this biggest intelligence coup of all time ... was thwarted in certain Foreign Office quarters "for fear of offending Russia"'*[42]

The second person I would single out from the very many who supplied intelligence to the British Secret Intelligence Service would be a man who to me seems to epitomize that Colville description of the Poles as the 'best all-round players'. Capt Roman Czerniawski, codename Armand, was one of a number of exiled Polish officers who in the wake of the Fall of France set up a series of intelligence networks there. The Interallié spy network that he founded in the second half of 1940 was centered on Paris but covered the whole of occupied France as well as parts of Belgium. Despite being a Polish network, it was truly multi-national, with the bulk of the agents being French but also including Poles, Belgians, Spaniards, Czechs and Germans. Messages were sent back to the UK. They were passed back to another Polish intelligence cell in southern France, according to the British documents, via Wagons-Lits attendants on the Paris to Marseilles express.[43] Interallié was by far the most significant network operating in occupied France. By October1941, it had more than 160 members and was passing back large numbers of reports on German troops and

---

[42] *Daily Telegraph* 30 May 1968, Wartime Head of the Secret Service Dies.
[43] Gill Bennett, France & North Africa, *The Report*....

their activities via a direct wireless link to the Polish Government-in-Exile in London. But then tragedy struck. The Germans arrested Czerniawski and rolled up the network. [44] But even now he turned the situation around, agreeing to go to England and work for the Germans as an agent-in-place, reporting back on allied preparations for the invasion of Europe. On his return to London, he told the authorities that he had been asked to spy for the Germans and under the codename Brutus was turned into one of the most effective of the double agents in the so-called Double Cross system.

The Double-Cross system originated from an MI5 plan based on an operation carried out by the French *Deuxième Bureau*. Dick White, a future head of both MI5 and MI6, suggested that captured agents of the German military intelligence service, the *Abwehr*, should be left in place and 'turned' to work as double agents for British intelligence. MI5 would be able to keep complete control over all German espionage activities in Britain and as a welcome side-effect, the information the agents asked for would tell the British what the *Abwehr* did and did not know. Initially, this was the full extent of MI5's ambitions. But it soon evolved into a major deception system; with agents feeding false information to the Germans that would provide allied plans with the best chance of success. [45]

At the Teheran Conference in November 1943, when the final decision was made to launch the invasion of Europe in mid-1944, Churchill told Stalin that 'in wartime, truth is so precious that she should always be attended by a bodyguard of lies'. From that point on, the overall deception plan for D-Day was known as Operation Bodyguard. By the beginning of 1944, the British were controlling 15 double agents, supposedly

[44] Rafał Wnuk, Polish Intelligence in France 1940-1945, *The Report*
[45] Michael Smith, Bletchley Park, Double Cross and D-Day, in *Action This Day*

collecting intelligence in the UK. Four of these were to be the key players in the deception plan to cover the actual D-Day landings, which was to be called Fortitude South under which the Germans were to be led to believe that the Normandy landings were a feint attack aimed at drawing German forces away from the main thrust of the allied invasion, which would be against the Pas de Calais. This would ensure that the bulk of the German forces would be held back from the Normandy beaches, allowing the Allies time to establish a strong foothold in northern France from which they could break out towards Paris and then on to the German border.

A completely mythical formation, the First United States Army Group (FUSAG), supposedly commanded by Gen George Patton, a hero of the invasion of Sicily and a man whom the Germans would believe must be heavily involved in the invasion of Europe, as indeed he later would. FUSAG was supposedly grouped in East Anglia and south-eastern England and it was vital that the agents' reports were coordinated to show that this was the case, and to downplay the mass of troops waiting in the south and south-west to attack the German defenses in Normandy. Brutus, who was supposedly a Polish liaison officer attached to FUSAG, provided an order of battle for the fictitious formation so detailed that the Germans were not just supplied with details of individual units, strengths and locations, but even with reproductions of the insignia painted on the side of their vehicles. [46]

There were four major agents, who in the parlance of the Double Cross Committee 'came up' for D-Day. Of these the most important was Garbo, the Spaniard Juan Pujol Garcia, whose reports were crucial in persuading the Germans that the attack would be against the Pas de Calais, persuading Hitler at the last minute to order two armoured divisions that had been

---

[46] R F Hesketh, Fortitude : The D-Day Deception Campaign, St. Ermins Press, London 1999.

sent to Normandy back towards Calais. But the second most important by far was Czerniawski /Brutus and it is worth noting that of the 208 German intelligence reports from that period that could be traced back to messages sent by the double agents, 91 came from Brutus compared to 86 from Garbo.[47]

I have selected just three star 'players' from among the many hundreds of Polish intelligence sources mentioned in this book. But we should remember that there were many more who do not get mentioned. We should also remember that these dry facts, important as they are in this joint effort to ensure that the contribution made by the Poles to the intelligence war is properly recognised, these dry facts cannot even begin to reflect the dangers that many of these brave men and women faced day after day.

> "No one could ever question of gallantry of your countrymen, either the armed forces or the civilians and I realise now, after having seen your men at war, why Poland will always survive – it is the courage of her people."
>
> (Maj.Gen. Colin McVean Gubbins, 19.11.1945)

---

[47] Ibidem

Clandestine inventions and devices, Poland's contribution in World War II

David List

'Nullius in Verba'

WHEN INVITED to give a paper on significant Polish inventions used during World War II to commemorate the 60th anniversary of it's ending, I hesitated at first. I was to speak to a bi-lingual audience of Polish war veterans and young generation of Poles born in Britain, gathered at the Polish Social and Cultural Centre in London. Nay I was disconcerted at the temerity of undertaking such a task; most especially as I am not a Polish speaker and my grasp of the Polish language comes with the aid of dictionary and the forbearance of many valued Polish friends. However, as I am an archival research specialist and the technical ingenuity of humanity is of great interest to me, I was prevailed upon to assist the 'fraternity at interest' who have laboured long, and mostly unsung, in the preparation of the first officially accredited Anglo-Polish history of Intelligence in World War II.[48] Together, with others of the international community of researchers and historians, I have long been annoyed and ashamed at the persistent inability of 'official historians' and particularly English language ones, to give due named recognition and credit to foreigners who may have, unpronounceable names; as the condescending quote from the

---

[48] *Intelligence Co-operation between Poland and Great Britain during World War II*, The Report of the Anglo-Polish Historical Committee, edited by Tessa Stirling, Daria Nałęcz, Tadeusz Dubicki, foreword by PM Tony Blair and PM Marek Belka, Vol.I, Valentine Mitchell, London 2005.

British official history 'SOE in France' demonstrates. Although, to be fair to the eminent Professor Michael Foot, the extant records of SOE[49] from which he drew his groundbreaking history, also give no mention whatever of the name, circumstance, rank, eminence, station or fate of the 'ingenious Pole' he alludes to:

'The H Type was the invention of an ingenious Pole who thought it inconvenient and dangerous to cart an object the size of a man, weighing over a tenth of a ton, round enemy territory.'

The published technical literature on patents attributed to the Poles as a whole is large, that in accessible English or, indeed, the Polish language and dealing with developments from 1939 to 1945 is negligible in either language, which is regrettable, because there is much of absorbing interest, which transcends the necessarily limited interests of wartime and the expeditious and least costly despatch of ones enemies. Amongst these I, personally, would number the development of miniaturised radio transmitter-receivers for clandestine service, collectively known by the nickname 'pipsztok' (pronounced 'peepshtock', most likely from the noise it makes, resembling a babbling child),[50] and whose etymology is - it is said, 'contested'. Among others: Methods of High Speed Radio Telegraphy; High Frequency/Direction Finding antenna types for use aboard warships, commonly called 'Huff Duff' after the written short form abbreviation 'HF/DF' used for this equipment. Not to mention, another Polish term with a 'contested' etymology - the 'Bombes' used for code breaking at Bletchley Park. The 'Mine Locator (Polish)' incontestably so named in British War Office approved documentation preserved at the United Kingdom's National Archives, and perhaps

---

[49] M.R.D. Foot, *SOE in France*, published in 1966, 1968 and 2004.
[50] Zbigniew Siemaszko, Polish Clandestine Radio in World War II, in periodical *Technika i Nauka,* (Technology & Science) No.72 2004.

surprisingly, the 'H' Type or skeleton parachute Container used for the clandestine delivery of stores to resistance groups and intelligence operators, world-wide. Others, no doubt, will have their own list of contenders and favourites for equally sound reasons. Amongst them might well be the intriguingly named 'Time Pencil' more prosaically designated the 'Switch No 10' from August 1943 to conform with the British Engineer designations.

I originally, gave this paper under the well-known Latin tag of *'Quo Warranto'* ('By whose authority?') since my information was based on, I hope, an informed study of the extant British public record made available to the world through that wonderful British institution, once known as the Public Record Office and now re-titled, in line with current style world-wide 'TNA' (The National Archives), which safeguards the records and institutional memory of central British government, going back to beyond the time of *Magna Carta* when the barons of England cried *'Quo Warranto'* of an oppressive monarch, in an unbroken chain of good custody which prevails because the now United Kingdom of Great Britain and Northern Ireland has not been successfully invaded by a hostile power since 1066 CE. Within that record and treasured memory is also, of course, a significant slice of the history of the Republic of Poland since these small islands became home to Poles escaping from the twin tyrannies of both Russia and Germany.

I have come to realise, more than ever, in considering the events and inventions, which simultaneously unite and divide our communities that the Latin motto *'Nullius in Verba'* of The Royal Society of London for the Improvement of Natural Knowledge, known more simply as the Royal Society (which claims to be the oldest learned society still in existence, since it was founded in 1660 CE). The Latin motto, (colloquially 'take nobody's word for it'; implication prove it by demonstration and evidence) is more fitting.

'The record' on which this exposition and that of many another published source rests is not one of authority and stature but more upon the shifting sands of apposite, elegant and appropriate language translation across cultures. In a large number of instances this is not achieved. A glance through both language versions of the official Report, already mentioned, the 'Time Pencil' is a case in point.[51] Professor Christopher Andrew another eminent British historian, writes, in his historical background of *The Report*: 'British-Polish Intelligence Collaboration during the Second World War in Historical Perspective':

'As chief of staff of the British military mission to Poland in the summer of 1939, Colin Gubbins (later Major-General and, from September 1943, executive director of SOE) brought back to London a device known as a time-pencil, capable of detonating plastic explosive after pre-set periods from ten minutes to thirty hours. Originally invented by the Germans during the First World War, improved by the Poles and perfected by the SOE's secret research establishment, Section X the time-pencil became a key part of SOE's sabotage armoury. More than twelve million of them were manufactured during the Second World War. [52]

Christopher Andrew and the triumvirate of editors of the aforementioned Report may not wish us to be confused and they, separately and collectively speak with due authority. Nevertheless, this statement is most certainly confusing, since 'Section X' was not 'SOE's secret research establishment' – but Station XII or Experimental Station VI (WD) at Aston House in Stevenage, Hertfordshire was.

---

[51] The National Archives (later TNA), HS 8/774

[52] *Intelligence Co-operation between Poland and Great Britain during World War II*, p.54. In the above quotation, Section X is not to be confused with Station X, a codename for Bletchley Park, Government Code and Cipher School Center.

The Germans did indeed devise an 'Incendiary Pencil' ie, a device based on an acid-chlorate delay principle, packaged within what appeared to be, to all intents and purposes, an ordinary propelling pencil but it wasn't 'improved by the Poles' and neither was it brought back to London by Gubbins as the attested archival paperwork of SOE at TNA demonstrates.[53] The English translation of the 'Protocol' of conversations held in Warsaw with Lt Col Gubbins and signed "Smoleński, płk dypl. Szef Oddz.II Sztab Główny", reads:

'In Poland experiments have been carried out with the 12 mm and 8 mm diameter Delay action fuses and according to the wish of Col Gubbins our suggestions have been made as to a more practical production. Models of the proposed corrections have been given. These corrections are indispensable on account of the standardisation of additional materials. Should the corrections we suggest be accepted in England as a basis of production we asked to manufacture for us, after indicating the prices: 500 x 12 mm diameter; 500 x 8 mm diameter fuse.'

Efforts to trace the original in Polish have, so far failed, although it is hoped that such might yet be found. What the document does demonstrate is that the Polish General Staff wanted to modify for their own demolition equipment and metric sizing, an existing British delay action fuze design, or switch, for which there are technical drawings, dated 31 April 1939, as well as supporting technical data in the public record transcripts of the British Royal Commission on Awards to Inventors sitting on 22 March 1954 to hear the case for John Langley to be recognised as the inventor of the crush action time delay design based on the properties of copper chlorate which featured at least four other novel and different features distinguishing his invention from the German device of the First

---

[53] TNA, HS 4/224, Protokół L 26125/11 dated 19 August 1939 of a conversation held in Warsaw 14-16 August between Lt.Col Gubbins and Col Smoleński Chief of the II (Intelligence) Bureau of the General Staff.

World War. I am indebted to Norman Bonney of Brunel University for his practical technical expertise and analysis of this topic which has long been wanting a proper historical study. Ironically, in our joint view, the misattribution of authorship results not from any original Polish claims, but comes from the writings of unwary British authors, as Christopher Andrew, so unfortunately continues to demonstrate.

Where Polish inventiveness is never in doubt is in the development by the radio engineer Józef Stanisław Kosacki, when a signals officer of I Korps in Scotland, in 1941, of an improved, electro-magnetic, non-contact device of some 28 lbs easily operable by one man for the location of buried land mines and other explosive charges with metal components, based on a model first invented in Poland in 1937. Using two magnetic coils producing an oscillating current from a portable battery pack which sounded as a continuous tone in headphones, adapted from pre-existing British signals equipment, the tone changed when the balance of the electro-magnetic field between the coils was disturbed by the presence of metal which could be as little as the oft quoted example of 'Shilling piece at 30 centimetres deep'. The British Army had no comparable equipment and first put it into production by the firm Cinema-Television Ltd in November 1941 as the 'Mine Locater (Polish) Model I'. The ensemble went through a continuous series of improvements in British Army service and as the Mine Detector (Polish) Model II [54] it was first used in significant numbers by the sappers of the Eight Army to clear the extensive minefields and booby trapping protecting the Italo-German forward defended localities in the El Alamein position in Libya on Operation Lightfoot in October 1942.

The design was never patented, either by Kosacki or by the Polish Government in Exile and no reward, except that of

[54] TNA, WO 199/1761; Polish Institute and Sikorski Museum holds on display the original Mine Detector no.3, ZA 22158.

recognition was ever sought. This latter came in the form of a letter of grateful thanks from the British Sovereign in due course. In practice, the continuous tone in the operators earphones was a design fault that could have been remedied because it caused so much operator fatigue, but the basic invention remained one of extensive utility, in use by all British (and indeed Polish) services and with some equipments being air dropped to resistance or airborne forces as needed. Only with the development by a Professor Rogowski of the Technische Hochshule, Aachen of the frequency 'induction igniter' deployed in limited quantities by the German Army in the last years of the war did the detectors supremacy over concealed metal-based munitions start to wane and even then, some models of the basic design remained in British service into the 1990s.[55]

The problem of air dropping stores by parachute from aircraft had been studied in a desultory fashion and a limited range of designs, usually based on bundling of existing stores packages in a number of webbing restraint harnesses had been developed for use by the RAF in aerial re-supply operations up to the outbreak of the Second World War when the development and deployment of airborne forces in both conventional and clandestine roles became of critical concern. Unlike Britain, Poland had a tiny airborne forces capability prior to the outbreak of the war based on equipment and expertise derived from the French, but does not appear, as far as the author has been able to ascertain, any equipment, design philosophy or expertise for the sustained and long-term re-supply of these forces from the air, although she had many unique designs of aviation equipment for the delivery of variable bomb loads onto tactical targets. Some of these designs, or improvements and variants of them by named and identifiable Polish inventors were subsequently

---

[55] TNA, WO 205/1180

adopted into RAF service on British built aircraft throughout the war and some of the literature gives unclear references to it.

Equipment for parachute aerial supply was developed by aviation and military research establishments in Britain basically to meet the needs of the British Army in open and overt warfare and only, almost as an afterthought, for clandestine operations, usually by night, by small groups of resistance fighters operating in hostile territory and with the need to easily conceal and man carry any small arms, explosives, equipment or rations delivered to them to places of safety before final distribution. Various designs, designated by letters of the alphabet, of large, heavy, metal streamlined container which could be easily carried and dropped from the bomb racks of British bomber aircraft were introduced into service, but it was only in 1942 that the requirements of resistance forces came to be addressed properly and this invaluable advance in the technology of clandestine resistance logistics, let alone the saving of muscle power by all concerned is simply attributed, when it is, to the invention of an anonymous 'Polish captain' as described by SOE's Air Operations Section, Containers officer, Major Harry Yelland, RE, who is the only primary source discovered by the writer to give an anyway detailed account of this life saver.[56]

The 'H' Type with a top payload weight of 235 lbs split down into five individual, nestable cells with a maximum possible payload of 73 lbs and a minimum of 41 lbs in each. Each cell came complete with its own carrying straps and provided tailored, portable loads that could be handled by single individuals or slung, pannier fashion, over any available beasts of burden. An alternative, but probably complementary account of the genesis of this Container design appears in an undated report [57] of unknown, but probably British, authorship dealing with the period 1942-1943, reads:

---

[56] TNA, HS 7/50
[57] TNA, HS 4/177

'The 'C' type in use during previous season [ie.1941-1942] found to be cumbersome and difficult to conceal. The idea was evolved of a container, which would break up into 5 cells, each cell light enough for 1 man to carry on the rucksack principle by means of straps. A Polish technical designer was found who put these ideas into practical form and after the necessary Air Ministry tests the current 'H' type container went into production - was used through the season with success.'

In the same file another, this time clearly Polish air liaison report, no 133, in English translation, dated 1 July 1942 makes similar suggests for a break down container design and is remarked upon in the transmittal note of 29 November 1942 from Maj. H.B. Perkins (MP) to Maj. Peter Wilkinson (MX), which covers it that 'the matter [is] already dealt with skeleton containers already in use'. Lastly, in another document [58] the 'H' Type container is said to be covered by a Polish patent, but there appears to be no British record of this and, as yet no Polish source has been traced to validate this claim. It appears to this writer that the lack of any identity for this anonymous 'Polish captain' or the 'Polish technical designer', who may well be one and the same person, should be one of interest, concern and investigation for Anglo-Polish historians; let alone the fact that there appears to be no extant Polish memorial, historical equipment display or commemoration of the individual or individuals and the life saving equipment they invented which deserves so well of both our countries in the fight for freedom. It is a project I commend to those more competent than I to undertake.

In the meantime, the adventurous will find that the Norwegians, whose SOE parachute trainees went through the parachute course together with the Poles, met and conquered

---

[58] TNA, HS 4/145

much the same problems of aerial supply as those in Poland have on display the 'H' Type in their resistance museum; but they, no more than we here, know of its inventor, and that too, is regrettable

"Nullius in Verba"

Polish Armoured Trains

Andrzej Suchcitz

> "Ever since Mr. Winston Churchill paid a visit 'to the Polish front', all the world has known that the army of Poland is in Scotland and is playing an operative part in its defence. It holds an important sector and the ardour, intelligence and skill that all ranks put into their military duties bode ill for the invader who should attempt to secure a footing in its neighbourhood. Between the Polish forces and those whom they would immediately defend a most friendly relationship has been established. It is a case of 'auld lang syne' for the exile soldiers and the Scottish people."
>
> (The Times, 13 May 1941)

THE FALL OF FRANCE in June 1940 brought imminent danger to the British Isles. The small British Expeditionary Force under General Lord Gort, miraculously evacuated from the beaches of Dunkirk, had to be re-equipped in preparation to ward of the expected German invasion (code name "Sealion"). For Great Britain every soldier and every piece of equipment saved from the French debacle was worth its weight in gold at the time. In all some 24,000 Polish troops (out of the 80,000 strong Polish Army in France) were evacuated from various ports in France to Britain. The majority were stationed in Scotland where soon the Polish I Corps was formed to take over the defence of Fife and Angus against a possible diversionary German landing, attempted from across occupied Norway. Whilst the air battle for Britain raged throughout the summer and early autumn of

1940, ground defences were being steadily organised, strengthened and built up. The War Office was literally prepared to try anything if only it would bolster the defence potential of Britain. As early as May 1940, Lt.Col. Adam Mount RE, the Chief Inspecting Officer of Railways at the Ministry of Transport, had suggested the creation of armoured trains as an additional means for the island's defence.[59] The War Office in London as well as the regional commands soon picked this up. One of the proposals sought approval, *"for the use of small armoured trains consisting of small tank engines with cattle trucks in front and rear. Trucks being sandbagged and loop holed with a Light Machine Gun and anti aircraft rifle in each truck. Approximate number of trains required [was] 20 for rapid reinforcement of points in lonely districts where communications were poor."*[60] Soon the War Office came up with the composition of the proposed trains.

In the centre was to be armour protected locomotive (built 1905-1910, mainly LNER Class F4). On either end of the locomotive was a platform, which was to be used for carrying essential supplies. At each end of the train were coal wagons each divided into two compartments. The end sections were mounted with 6 pounder Hotchkiss type II guns. This was an old gun used in tanks dating from the 1 World War when it had been adapted from an 1885 naval gun. It was regarded as an anti-tank weapon effective at 800 to 1000 yards. The other compartment had three Bren light machine guns for use against enemy infantry. Each train was also armed with two "Boys" anti tank rifles. The two end trucks were reinforced with an internal armoured lining between which and the original truck plating

---

[59] G.Balfour, *The Armoured Train. Its development and usage.* London 1981, p.65

[60] The National Archives (TNA), WO166/115, note from June 1940 on the organisation of armoured trains.

there was a four inch thick cement wall. Cement was used due to a lack of armour plating. A detailed technical sketch of the armoured train was later prepared by Lt.Stefan Majde, Technical Officer 1st Armoured Train Group at Brentwood in May 1942 (see illustration). This provides information about the total arms and ammunition carried, the intercommunication system as well as the coal and water supplies needed to operate the trains.

Twelve such trains were formed each with a crew of 1 officer, 7 NCOs and 47 other ranks, 39 from the Royal Armoured Corps and 8 from the Royal Engineers. This was a full complement of 55 soldiers besides the driver, fireman and brakeman. From a tactical point of view the trains were subordinated to the local divisional or more often brigade commanders in the areas they were operating. From an administrative stand point four armoured train groups were established each with two or more trains. Initially the trains were numbered 1 to 12, though they were soon renamed A to M (with the letter I being missed out). The main task of the armoured trains was the patrolling of coastal lines on the southern and eastern seaboards of the United Kingdom. Patrolling was carried out mainly at dawn though also during daylight hours. However patrols had to be carried out so as not to disrupt the passenger or freight train timetables. This created some humorous moments for the armoured trains, which were supposedly on active service. The fact, that the rail services were privatised and divided regionally added to the running difficulties, especially if the patrol route of a train took it across two regions. The armoured trains were to help fight off an airborne landing and support ground troops defending against a sea borne invasion. The first patrol made by a British armoured train was carried out on 7 July 1940.

Meanwhile the Polish Army evacuated to Scotland was facing manning difficulties. There was a preponderance of officers over other ranks. This meant that apart from two brigades at near or full strength the remainder of the ground formations had to be organised on a cadre basis. Even so there were still many officers for whom there was no active employment. In the summer of 1940 the elderly Colonel Mikołaj Kolankowski, a sometime commander of a Military Railway Regiment in the 1920s, put forward the idea of using surplus Polish officers to man the armoured trains, thus releasing British personnel for other duties. He was soon appointed Commandant of the Polish Armoured Forces Base and tasked with preparing crews for twelve trains.[61] The only proviso was that no officers were to be drawn from 3rd, 4th or 5th Cadre Rifle Brigades, which formed part of the defence forces of Scotland. Meantime, agreement on this was soon reached by British and Polish staffs in London. As a result on 17 September 1940 the Polish Commander-in-Chief, General Władysław Sikorski, issued an order confirming the organisational structure and manning of the twelve trains.[62] The Polish crews took over the trains in several phases between October 1940 and February 1941, though in most cases the period of take over lasted several weeks longer if not more.

The first to be taken over by the Poles were trains 10, 11 and 12 (soon renamed J, L and K), which formed 4th Armoured Train Group under Col.Kazimierz Alexandrowicz (later Lt-Col.Józef Szyłejko and Col.Aleksander Batory). Group HQ was moved from Stirling to Perth. These trains were to be used in support of Polish forces defending Fife and Angus and unlike the remaining groups was subordinated to the General Officer

---

[61] Andrzej Suchcitz, Pociągi pancerne w Wielkiej Brytanii 1940-1943, in *Pociągi pancerne 1918-1943 (Armoured Trains 1918-1943) Organizacja-struktura-działania wojenne*, ed. by U.Kraśnicka and K.Filipow, Białystok 1999, p.58.

[62] Instytut Polski i Muzeum gen. Sikorskiego (Polish Institute and Sikorski Museum) later as IPMS, A.VI.25/1, Organisation of Armoured Trains, 17 September 1940

Commanding Polish Its Corps, General Marian Kukiel. In November trains C, G and E under Col.Leonard Łodzia-Michalski forming 1st Group were taken over. Their patrol area were the counties of East Anglia, expanding later to take in Kent. At one time this group had five armoured trains. The 3rd Group (trains B, M and H) under Col.Józef Kapciuk began to take over its trains in January 1941, though it was not until March that this had been completed and the British crews finally withdrawn. The area of patrol was the north eastern counties of England. This group was soon reduced to two trains as Train H was moved to Canterbury and eventually formally transferred to 1st Group. In February Polish crews began taking over 2nd Group (trains A, D and F) under Lt-Col Adam Zbijewski. This group patrolled the Devon and Cornwall coasts.[63] 1st, 2nd and 3rd Groups came under the administrative command of the Second General for Special Duties of the Minister of War, Tactical command was held by the local British divisional and brigade commanders in whose areas the trains operated. The planned replacing of the friver, firman and brakeman with Polish personnel was however shelved and these functions remained in British hands.

Compared with the pre war Polish armoured trains these small ad hoc trains must have been seen as something of a joke. As one officer noted: *"Those who had seen Polish armoured trains back home and knew their armament and fire power would be sorely disappointed here".* Another officer commented on the armament. *"The gun – like a gun. From my first look, very similar to those my father had shown me on the walls of Częstochowa monastery [from the 17th century]...First impressions were very negative. We know the English only a little as yet... At this moment they seem not lacking in a sense of humour.... Due to a lack of modern arms they have taken out*

---

[63] A.Suchcitz, in *Pociągi pancerne..*, p.59-61

CONTAINERS, "H" TYPE
Catalogue No. 15C 170.

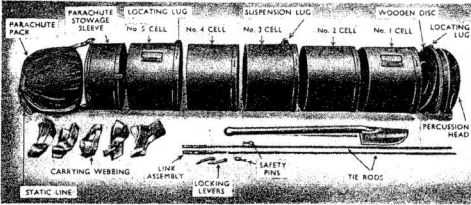

LAYOUT OF CONTAINER COMPONENTS

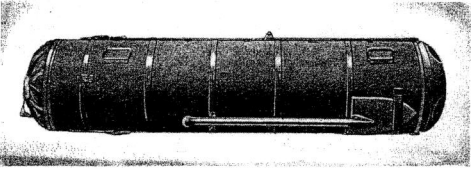

CONTAINER READY FOR ATTACHMENT TO AIRCRAFT

"H" type Polish Container drawing, showing its various components

Distinctive "H" type Container (middle view) ready for transport

Photographs

The Polish Mine Detector
(instruction sheet).

A Polish sapper at work with the
Mine Detector

Armoured Train in Scotland at a stop of a country station

Armoured Train D at Manningtree, Essex 25.3.1942

Two Polish Armoured Trains ready for an assignment

Inspection time of the Armoured Train and crew by the British officers

Soldiers on parade with Scottish pipers on Polish Army Day
15 August 1940

A Polish Ambulance Column run by the Women's Auxiliary Service

*Three riflemen from the Independent Parachute Brigade
aiming at the enemy*

*Polish gunners manning a coastal defence
(a charge is being thrown up to the gun crew's loading number for
placing into the breech of the 6 inch gun).*

Polish gunners in operation

Polish soldiers working on the construction of an anti-barrage device on the eastern coast of Scotland

Polish soldiers of the 10 Mounted Rifles Regiment working on coastal fortifications, Arbroath 1941

Lt Col K. Maresch being presented to Gen. Field Marshall Alan Brooke

from under the undergrowth some old junk. The whole made an impression, which can be summed up in one sentence: This is a combat unit which will not frighten the enemy and will impress those persons who have not seen a modern armoured train."[64]
The same author also described a typical patrol.
'We are ready' shouts the engine driver leaning out of his cab. Somebody replies 'All right' ... the voice of our commander taken up with his mission is lost in all the terrible noise and acrid smoke as he shouts 'Attention, attention - Action Stations'. We had hardly left the station when a gale blew up dislodging helmets from the crew, made up of know it all artillerymen, disdainful cavalrymen, cantankerous infantrymen, reliable engineers and the unconcerned and always cheerful signalmen. We did not meet the enemy - everywhere the harmonious English monotony, peace and uniformity. People we passed along the route stretched out their arms and gave the thumbs up sign, which supposedly signified victory (sic). They never lost their spirit and confidence. We returned [to base] after several hours wet and black from the soot".[65]

The Polish armoured train's fiercest exponent was Col Łodzia-Michalski commanding 1st Group in East Anglia and Kent. In spring 1941 he had put forward a whole series of proposals which, "related mainly to the trains' armament and included the provision of two Vickers medium machine guns for each train and an anti-aircraft mounting for a Bren gun in the centre of each main fighting compartment. For fighting at close quarters Michalski sought a quantity of hand grenades and two Thompson machine guns for each train, while for demolition purposes he advocated carrying twenty pounds of high explosives together with the necessary fuses and detonators.

---

[64] J.Pietrzycki, Jak to na wojence..... różnie, in *Przegląd Kawalerii i Broni Pancernej* no.52, October-December 1968, London, p.267
[65] Op.cit. p.268

Small modifications designed to increase the effectiveness of the train's fire power were proper mountings for the Vickers guns and anti-tank rifles, and a general increase in ammunition scales".[66] Many of these proposals were gradually implemented though with scale differences according to their availability. Only some trains received the Vickers guns but on the other hand all received four instead of two Thompson's. Ammunition allocations were increased though there was no extra ammunition available for the main armament. An idea to replace the 6 pounder with either a 75mm or 18 pounder field gun came to nothing. Certain modification to strengthen the armour of the train, for example the locomotive boiler and the protective shield around the 6 pounder were gradually implemented, whilst other protective ideas did not find favour either with the War Office or the railway authorities. Eventually the trains received an additional armoured tender increasing the water capacity and so facilitating additional cruising range and also braking power. To improve the tactical capabilities of the train in combat conditions and reducing its reliance on its home base, Col.Łodzia-Michalski proposed that the supply base of each train be made mobile; reducing the need for trains to constantly return to their bases to replenish supplies.

„This mobile base consisting of a passenger coach and a covered van "would be attached to the rear of the train when it left its base and would be detached at a convenient place some miles in the rear of the intended scene of action. At night the train would return to the mobile base, whose site would be chosen with regard to the need to take on coal and water."[67]

In essence this idea was approved and implemented. 4th Group was first to attain combat readiness and in November

---

[66] G.Balfour, *The Armoured Train*, p.13

[67] Op.cit. p.131

1940 received its first operational instructions. For example Armoured Train 10 patrolling the line Edinburgh – Montrose and Montrose – Perth – Edinburgh, was to support the coastal defence where the terrain made this possible, support the left flank of Polish Ist Corps, maintain liaison with British units and co-operate in the defence of vulnerable points along the railway line as identified by the British commanders. Throughout 1941 the armoured trains maintained a steady level of activity, averaging 3 to 4 patrols weekly. During the summer months alone the twelve trains carried out over 100 patrols. On the whole the routes patrolled remained constant. Thus for example from March 1942 Train B patrolled the north east coast of England along the line north of Tweedmouth – Alnmouth – Chevington – Morpeth – Newcastle. Along this stretch it had six specific patrol routes. Earlier it has participated in 9th Corps exercises along the route between Tweedmouth and Coldstream along the river Tweed. The second train of 3rd Group, Train M based at Spalding had routes covering Lincolnshire from Peterborough in the south, Kings Lynn in the east, northwards through Spalding to Firsby, Skegness, Grimsby and New Holland on the Humber. In south west England Train D stationed at Wadebridge in Cornwall carried out patrols to Padstow and Port Isaac Road as well as further trips to Newton Abbot and Barnstaple. Train A stationed at Newton Abbot in Devon patrolled routes between Exeter and Kingswear, whilst Train F operated in the Barnstaple area. Following the transfer of Train D from 2nd to 1st Group in the summer of 1941, the home base of Train D, which took over this stretch in addition to its own, was moved to St.Austell.

Tactically subordinated to local commands it was not until May 1941 that the individual trains had an opportunity to participate in British army exercises at brigade and divisional level. For the Polish General Staff the existence of Polish manned armoured trains was to be a passing phase. The ultimate aim was for these officers to be used in armoured formations, which were to be created. Thus the main emphasis was laid on as many officers as possible undergoing various courses connected with motorisation and armoured warfare and being sent on detachment to British armoured units.[68] Individual train commanders requested from their divisional commanders the use of vehicles and motorcycles so that the crews could begin to carry out the necessary training and schooling. Courses were laid on at the district workshops and at various specialist centres.

In their three year career on British soil, Polish armoured trains were thrice involved, albeit indirectly with enemy actions, all as a result of German bombing raids. On 8th November 1941 some billets of Train B's crew were destroyed at Alnmouth. Luckily the Train was on a patrol and there were only three slightly wounded amongst the Polish soldiers. However eight civilians were killed. During the night of 31 May/1 June 1942 Canterbury suffered an air raid, which killed forty of its citizens. Some billets and the supply park of Train H were hit causing fires and the destruction of one tank and the damage of another. The fire was put out due to the presence of mind and bravery of Lt.Józef Tomankiewicz, but one of the crew, Lt.Kokoszko died from wounds received. On 23 March 1943 the crew of Train E of 2nd Group helped in the rescue work following a bombing raid on Ashford in Kent. The crew received many acknowledgements from the town for their rescue effort.[69]

A central feature of the work of the armoured trains was not military but cultural, namely the promotion of Anglo-Polish understanding. For the majority of the local inhabitants this was their first encounter with foreigners and from an exotic and unknown place such as Poland! Language barriers were partially overcome by constant English lessons, but above all by the

---

[68] IPMS, C.54, War Diary of 3rd Armoured Train Group, p.7
[69] A.Suchcitz, in *Pociągi pancerne*, p.65

many concerts, dances, exhibitions and lectures promoting
Poland and its culture. The train crews organised charity
concerts and events, the proceeds going either to local
organisations or national ones such as the British Red Cross.
Local libraries and school libraries became the recipients of
books in English on Poland, its literature and way of life. These
were purchased by donations from the train crews. The
commander of Train E in Tonbridge wrote that when they
arrived they had been received coolly. After four months they
were bade a fond farewell by the whole population.[70] Many of
the towns, which were the home bases of the armoured trains,
received memorial plaques, whilst Roman Catholic churches
received religious iconography with special dedications. Thus
for example St.Pancras RC Church in Ipswich received a
painting of Our Lady Of Częstochowa from the crew of
Armoured Train C.

As has been noted previously the manning of the
armoured trains by Polish crews was seen as a temporary
measure. The main aim of the Polish General Staff, apart from
obviously maximising the active participation of Polish Forces
in the defence of Britain, was to use this period for the intensive
training of the officer crews in motorised and armoured warfare
so that at the appropriate time they could take up new
commissions in the armoured divisions and brigades which were
to be formed.

In the autumn of 1941 the Polish command structure of
the Armoured Trains was reorganised and a unified Inspectorate
of Armoured Trains was set up which was subordinated to the
Ist General for Special Duties of the Commander-in-Chief and
then directly to the Chief of General Staff. The erstwhile
Commanding Officer 1st Group Col.Łodzia-Michalski took up

---

[70] IPMS, C.55/IV, War Diary of Armoured Train E. Major Dobkiewicz's
report to the Head of the Propaganda and Education Department, Polish
General Staff, 26 June 1941

the post of Inspector on 1st November 1941. A month later he had successfully obtained from the C-in-C Home Forces agreement for the addition of four Bren carriers for each train. Due to other demands on them, they did not start arriving until spring 1942. Michalski's hope to obtain flat platforms to carry them came to nothing as they were in much demand elsewhere. Thus as the historian G.Balfour wrote, the Bren carriers *"would operate on the ground in association with the trains, very much as cavalry had done in South Africa forty years before."*[71]

On 12 January 1942 Polish GHQ submitted to Gen. Paget the new C-in-C Home Forces a request to withdraw the Polish train crews, which were now needed for Polish Forces being organised and trained in Britain, the USSR and the Middle East. The idea was that Home Guard units would gradually replace Polish crews. To ease the transition and provide time to find the necessary replacement crews Col.Michalski offered to stagger the reduction of the crews being also aware that they could not all be absorbed automatically into the new armoured units being formed. However he insisted that the Polish trains be grouped in Eastern or South Eastern Commands, which had the best facilities for *"training in association with British armoured formations"*.[72] The first train to be handed over was Train B from 3rd Group in north east England in April 1942. In the summer of that year 4th Group in Scotland was handed over to the British and soon after the remaining Train M of 3rd Group, operating between Kings Lynn and the Humber was also taken over by the British. The remaining trains of 2nd Group in south west England were transferred to the south east. More importantly, by the summer of 1942 the remaining seven Polish Armoured Trains had received not only their Bren carriers (four

---

[71] G.Balfour, *The Armoured Train,* p.138
[72] Op.cit. p.142

to a train) but also armoured Bedford trucks (three to a train) and Covenanter and Valentine tanks. Life revolved around regular patrols, though these decreased during 1942 and 1943 and above all intensive armoured training.

In March 1943 came the final decision to withdraw all the Polish crews. This was steadily carried out to September that year. The last trains to be handed over were Train D at Manningtree in late August/early September and Train H in mid September at Ashford. The last exercise in which a Polish train participated was Exercise "Rainbow" in April 1943. This was Armoured Train D operating from Manningtree. It is worth quoting in full the report of Captain I.A.M.MacLennan of the 1st Battalion the Highland Regiment attached to the Train with two officers and two NCO umpires as apart from the somewhat Dada Army feeling about it provides a good insight into how the armoured trains operated and the problems they encountered. In his report he noted:

"17.4.43, 16.30: reported to Polish HQ with 2 Officer and 2 NCO Umpires;17.00: Handed first message from Colchester Garrison to OC. No action was taken, as OC then understood from Area HQ that he was not required to take part in the exercise until 06.00 hrs on 18.4.43.

18.4.43, 06.00: Handed second message to OC. Plan decided upon; 06.04: Orders issued to OC Carrier detachment.

06.07: Carrier detachment on the move. Orders issued by their officer; 06.08: HQ left for train; 06.14: Train actually ready to move off – orders have been issued.

06.30: Train left station – time having been allowed for Carrier screen to move ahead. Wireless contact established with Czech Brigade. Contact NOT made with Carriers as one valve was blown in R/T set and no spare was carried.

06.40: Message by telephone from Carriers picked up at Station.

06.50: Message from Czech Bde – by telephone – asking for W/T contact; this had already been done;

06.55: Carrier Number left at contact point, signalled "No enemy in sight" 07.00: Train stopped and reconnaissance patrol sent out from train; 07.10: Train stopped at PRIORY HALT, where it remained until the conclusion of the Exercise.

Remarks:

a) *Language was at times a problem, especially at critical times in the operation, but on the whole a judicious mixture of various languages served*

b) *The Polish O.C. quite clearly understood that he was NOT to move until the morning of the 18th, therefore saw no reason to take action on receipt of the first message. [17.00 hours, 17 April 1943] We attempted to persuade him to "Stand-to" but he was more successful in persuading us to have dinner instead! A "Stand-to" he said would take only twenty minutes.*

c) *The action on receipt of the second message [06.00 hours, 18th April 1943]*

d) *Radio communication was not reliable on this occasion. Contact was not maintained with the Carriers, who were completely in the blue after the first bound. Although on this particular occasion communication with the outside world was fairly reasonable one could all to easily visualise that in actual battle things would not have run so smoothly. This seems to be a real problem in a train of this sort where communication is extremely and dependent solely on R/T.*

e) *The quietness and speed with which this unit got down to essentials from the operational viewpoint was most notes worthy and others could well emulate their example. The patrol referred to above left the train, opened out and searched the ground without any noise occurring at any stage. The Commander's orders were given out in two sentences, the patrol leader replied in one sentence and spoke one further sentence to his patrol. And that was ALL. The whole operation was carried out at great speed and without regard to personal comfort! It was altogether an excellent bit of work.*

f) At PRIORY HALT, I was faced with two alternatives: -

    i) To wait for 50 minutes while various trains passed us – there was ½ mile of single track at this point.

    ii) To go on to somewhere beyond PARKSTONE where we would lie in a siding. We had to get there in 12 minutes.

The Polish C.O. did not favour either course as (b) was obviously no use at all from the tactical point of view and (a) meant a late arrival. I ordered him to wait at the HALT as I hoped thereby to arrive in the main battle at a fairly interesting stage. At any rate by staying there I would avoid the no doubt inspiring but nevertheless somewhat farcical spectacle of an armoured train careering through the thick of a battle at a fairly rapid rate, without regard for either friend or foe, heading for an obscure siding some miles further on. There had already been some rather light-hearted moments in which an RE corporal who apparently owned the train, insisted, despite a certain linguistic difficulty o, on progress in time-table rather than tactical fashion, as we were apparently being pursued hotly by the local passenger train. Various people were by this time laughing in fairly hysterical fashion and this last dash I felt to be more than anyone should fairly be asked to endure.

g) The Carriers were split – 2 sections of 2 machines – for the first part of the distance, linking up again on the road WEST of STOUR WOOD. Their plan was certainly a bold one but on the other hand it was about the only thing they could do. It was carried out fairly well. The main criticism of the Umpires who were with them was that a certain amount of thoughtlessness tended to lead them into situations, which would, to say the least, have been unpleasant in actual war.

h) *Finally I would like to stress that the Senior Umpire's remarks with regard to Polish hospitality should be treated with the seriousness, which they undoubtedly deserve. They did however arrange that I spent a comfortable night in an hotel bed!"* [73]

On 3 August 1943 the new Polish C-in-C General Kazimierz Sosnkowski issued a farewell order to the Polish Armoured Train crews in which thanking them and paying tribute to their work he summarised their achievements which apart from having contributed to the defence strength of the British Isles had resulted in some 600 officers having undergone various specialist course with Polish units and 450 with British units. Over 100 concerts, 200 lectures, 150 film shows had been organised up and down the country bringing Poland closer to the local population. Some 100 local and school libraries had received gifts of books on Poland.[74] A few days earlier the Inspector of Armoured Trains had issued his own farewell order to 1st Group in which whilst recognising the difficult conditions in which the crews had worked believed

"that the officers had understood his ideas and intentions: not to waste any of the human resources that they represented – the road through training led to being ready for new tasks, ready for the modern mechanised Polish Army.... The Polish Army had gained many valuable specialists and

[73] IPMS, C.55/III, War Diary Armoured Train D. Report by umpire with "D" Armoured Train – Exercise Rainbow, 19 April 1943.

[74] IPMS, C.55/IV War Diary of Train E. C-in-C's Order No.11 of 3 August 1943

instructors needed now and in the future for the creation of modern mechanised formations".[75]

To commemorate the service of the Polish Armoured Trains a special badge was approved by the Polish C-in-C in late 1941, which was awarded to the crews. It represented the Polish hussars helmet above a ribbon on which were written the place names: "Essex, Devon, York and Perth". The last chapter in the distinguished history of Polish Armoured Trains had closed on British soil – one of the least known chapters of the Polish Army's role in the defence of the United Kingdom.

---

[75] Op.cit, Col.L.Łodzia-Michalski to CO 1st Armoured Train Group, Lt-Col.M.Kotarba

The Polish Army as part of the Defence Forces of Scotland 1940-1945

Zbigniew Wawer and Andrzej Suchcitz

> "I was very glad to see the Polish Forces in Scotland. Their smart and resolute bearing convinced me that when the call for action comes, they will confirm the reputation for soldierly and audacious bravery which they and they comrades have already won on the battlefields of Poland, France and Norway. Poland has shed her blood in that same cause of Right of Freedom for which we in England are fighting now in the hour of her misfortune …"

> (Winston Churchill to Gen. Sikorski, 27 October 1940)

FOLLOWING THE DEFEAT OF FRANCE in June 1940 the Polish Commander-in-Chief, Gen. Władysław Sikorski took steps to recreate the Polish Army for a second time. As a consequence of unwritten Anglo-Polish agreements made on 19 June, Polish Forces were to be evacuated to Great Britain. From 24 June Polish units started arriving on British soil. Polish forces evacuated to Britain were first located in make shift army camps south east of Glasgow, at Coatbridge (remnants of the 3rd Infantry Division), Broughton (remnants of the 4th Infantry Division), Ballahouston (remnants of the Independent Highland Rifle Brigade) and Glasgow (remnants of the 10th Motorised Cavalry Brigade and some central institutions. By the end of June, 1863 officers and 10449 other ranks of the Polish Army had been accounted for on the British Isles.[76] Gen. Sikorski had hoped to evacuate at least 23,000 men from whom he planned to organize two infantry brigades and an armoured brigade as well as reinforcing the Polish Air Force.[77]

Following the defeat of France the Germans began preparing the invasion of Britain. The British began to organise new formations for the island's defence. This also had an effect on the future organisation of the Polish Armed Forces based in Britain. At the beginning of July 1940 the Polish army units, which had been evacuated from France were moved to Biggar (remnants of 3 and 4 Infantry Divisions), Douglas (remnants of 10th Motorised Cavalry Brigade and of the Independent Highland Brigade) Crawford (engineers, signals and anti aircraft artillery). Gen.Dreszer, Col.Glabisz and Gen.Paszkiewicz were appointed respective commanders, whilst the remaining soldiers were grouped in camps around Peebles and the surplus officers were located in officer camps near Broughton and in Rothesay on the Island of Bute.[78] On 5 July 1940 all Polish camps in Scotland were subordinated to the General Officer Commanding Polish Army Camps and Units in Scotland.[79] A week later, on 13 July the 1st Rifle Brigade was formed under the command of Gen. Paszkiewicz. A few days later the 2 Rifle Brigade began formation under Gen. R.Dreszer. An Armoured Group was formed simultaneously.

---

[76] Instytut Polski i Muzeum gen. Sikorskiego (Polish Institute and Sikorski Museum) later as IPMS, KOL.1/DCNW/June1940:Gen.Sikorski's War Diary.
[77] IPMS, KOL.1/DCNW/ 28 June 1940.
[78] *Polskie Siły Zbrojne w drugiej wojnie światowej* (*The Polish Armed Forces in World War Two* – further cited as PSZ), Vol.I, part 2, London 1959 p.239; Zakład Historyczny Ruchu Ludowego (ZHRL), Prof.Kot Archives folio 148, Report for the C-in-C.
[79] The GOC of these units was Lt-Gen.Stanisław Burhardt-Bukacki (1890-1942).

At the beginning of August Gen. Marian Kukiel replaced Gen. Stanisław Burhardt-Bukacki as GOC Polish Camps and Units in Scotland.[80]

Meanwhile on 5 August 1940 in London, the Anglo-Polish Military Agreement was signed by Winston Churchill and Lord Halifax (Secretary of State for Foreign Affairs) on the one hand, and Gen. Sikorski and August Zaleski (Polish Foreign Minister) on the other. In fact this agreement was in breach of British constitutional law, which forbade the existence of a foreign army on British soil without the consent of the British Parliament. Despite this and because of the threat to the British Isles the British Prime Minister and his Foreign Secretary signed the agreement. The stay of Polish Forces on British soil was legalised on 22 August 1940 by the passing of the Allied Forces Act, which gave the Polish Armed Forces similar rights to those enjoyed by the British and Commonwealth Forces. The agreement stipulated that the Polish Land Army would form a single operational formation, operating in a single operational theatre, under the command of its own commanders, under Polish colours and external badges and insignia. In certain circumstances these units could be subordinated to British command, as long as the Polish command gave its approval. The Polish Forces were to be kitted out and supplied by Britain and Polish troops were to be answerable to the Polish judiciary and in exceptional circumstances to British criminal law.[81] The Anglo-Polish Agreement allowed for the formation of new units in Scotland. Because there were too few troops and an abundance of officers it was decided to organise cadre brigades, which would expand to full strength with the arrival of Polish troops escaping from France.

---

[80] Ibidem

[81] Z.Wawer, *Organizacja Polskich Wojsk Lądowych w Wielkiej Brytanii 1940-1945* (The organisation of the Polish Land Army in Great Britain 1940-1945), Warsaw 1992, p.37-38.

Between August 1940 and February 1941 the 3rd, 4th, 5th, 7th and 8th Cadre Rifle Brigades were formed which for the defence of the Scottish coast against invasion were organised into officer battalions.[82] On 28 September 1940 the Polish Commander-in-Chief, Gen.Sikorski issued an order forming out of the above units and the 1st Rifle Brigade, the Ist Polish Corps in Scotland.[83] In part this was a political decision to underline that the Polish Army in Britain, numbering some 20,000 troops was far larger than that of the other allied powers such as Norway, Czechoslovakia, Holland and Belgium. Gen.Sikorski also had his eye on the future expansion of the corps into an army composed of several corps.[84] Gen.Marian Kukiel was appointed Gen. Officer Commanding I Corps, whilst corps HQ was formed from the old HQ of Polish Camps and Units in Scotland.

On 8th October 1940 the corps' organisation was established as consisting of: HQ, Reconnaissance Squadron, Medium Artillery Battery, Tank Regiment, Signals Company, Engineers Battalion, two motorised columns including an ambulance once, three depots, Military Hospital nr.1 at Taymouth, Military Hospital No.2 at Cessnach Castle, Central Training Camp at Crawford and above all the operational units forming two rifle brigades and three cadre rifle brigades.[85]

With the ever increasing threat of a German invasion of the British Isles, the War Office decided already in August 1940

---

[82] S.Sosabowski, *Droga wiodła ugorem* (*An uphill struggle*), London 1967, p.102-103; T.Kryska Karski, J.Bahrynowski, S.Żurakowski, *Piechota Polska* (Polish Infantry) part 9-10, p.77, 82 and 88; PISM, A.VI.3/1 Ordre de Bataille 3rd Cadre Rifle Brigade.

[83][83] IPMS, A.XII.22/87, Organizacja wojenna i ich realizacja, 26 September 1940.

[84] IPMS, KOL.1/DCNW/26 October 1940, App.1, p.1

[85] IPMS, A.XII.22/87, Documeny no.L.dz.788/tjn, 8 October 1940 p.1-4, Changes to the organisation of Polish I Corps.

that the recently arrived Polish Forces would be used in the defence of the eastern coast of Scotland, where it was envisaged that a diversionary German landing from Norway may take place, whilst the main landings would come across the Channel on the southern coast of England.[86] Polish forces numbering some 14,000 men (of which 3,500 were officers) forming Polish I Corps would take over a 200 kilometre sector from Firth of Forth in the south to a point south of Montrose in the north.[87] This encompassed Fife and Angus. The most vulnerable beaches to a landing covered a length of 30 kilometres. The line between the Firth of Forth and Firth of Clyde formed the narrowest part of Scotland, which could easily be cut in two here, cutting off the northern naval bases and leaving the enemy in control of the industrial area around Glasgow. The main area of possible concern was the Rosyth Naval Base and the airbases at Donibristle, Leuchars and New Scone on the southern coast of the Firth of Forth as well as the city of Dundee on the Firth of Tay.[88]

It was accepted by the planners that the defence forces must defeat the enemy on the beaches and prevent him from establishing bridgeheads. At the same time the possibility of air assaults was taken into account. The defence forces were to be grouped on a wide front and in depth, with strong mobile reserves, which could be used in the most endangered areas as and when necessary. In the summer of 1940 the 46th Infantry Division and various training units defended this sector. On 21 September 1940 Scottish Command under Lieutenant-General Robert Carrington issued orders laying out the tasks for amongst

---

[86] PSZ, Vol.II, Part 1, p.245-246. The initial decisions concerning the use of I Corps in the defence of the Scottish coast were taken in August 1940, though it was not until October that the defensive positions were taken up.

[87] PSZ, Vol.II, Part 1, p.248-249

[88] The National Archives (TNA), WO 166/116, Scottish Command Defence Scheme.

others the Polish Forces, which were to seek and destroy any enemy operating in its sector. British units were to operate under the local Area Commanders, working through their Sub-Area Commanders. As the orders stated

"An exception to this is the case of the Polish Forces. These will operate as an independent force under their own commander, under the direct control of the GOC-in-C Scottish Command. Liaison between the Polish Forces and neighbouring formations as well as with all civilian authorities will be maintained through existing British Area and Sub-Area Commanders".[89]

The distribution of Polish I Corps was such that one brigade (1st Independent Rifle Brigade under Gen. G. Paszkiewicz) was to defend Fife; a second brigade (10th Motorised Cavalry Brigade under Gen.S.Maczek) was to defend Angus with a smaller force of battalion strength at Dumfermline to intervene at Rosyth and Donibristle.

Whilst the local Home Guard Battalions and coastal defences in the area were not subordinated to the Polish I Corps, the 151st Light Artillery Regiment and several artillery troops in the St.Andrews area were operationally under the Polish commander. As its neighbours the Poles had the 51st Division to the north and first the 46th, later the 52nd Division to the south. The corps commander Gen.Marian Kukiel issued his detailed defence orders on 12 October with full disposition of units. A week later he took over full operational control of his defence sector. His HQ was located at Moncrieff House near Bridge of Earn, south of Perth. His corps numbered 3,498 officers and 10,884 other ranks. At the time Gen.Carrington wrote to Gen. Kukiel: " *I am certain that the units under your command will continue the noble tradition of the Polish Army[...] I know, that if the need arises, the units under Your command, linked in arms*

---

[89] ibidem.

with the British units will defend British soil with the same duty and dedication".[90]

In October 1940 the Polish sector was visited by the British Prime Minister Winston Churchill and Gen.Sikorski. Six weeks later the General Officer Commanding-in-Chief Home Forces, Gen.Alan Brooke visited I Corps, inspecting the defences at Dundee. He voiced his high opinion of the readiness of 5ᵗʰ Cadre Rifle Brigade defending this sector. An exhausted Brooke wrote in his diary:

"Arrived at 6.45 am in Dundee, freezing hard and very cold! Bath and breakfast in the hotel and then reception of Kukiel (Commander of Polish Forces) and Sikorski, followed by Guard of Honour of Poles outside the hotel and then continuous guards of honour, marches past, salutes and inspections and introductions from 9am to 6pm!!"[91]

However the visit did convince Brooke of the value of the cadre brigades over which the British staffs to date were sceptical.[92] Gen.Lanuge commanding the British artillery in the region reported to the War Office on the high quality training and preparedness of the Polish artillery.

The disposition of the I Corps made in October 1940 remained basically unchanged to the spring of 1941. Fife was defended by 1ˢᵗ Independent Rifle Brigade and the 4ᵗʰ Cadre Rifle Brigade (later the 1ˢᵗ Independent Airborne Brigade which distinguished itself at Arnhem). The battalions of the 1ˢᵗ Brigade were based at Tents Muir beaches, Leuchers airfield, St.Andrews and the coast to the south east, whilst 4ᵗʰ Cadre Brigade under Col.S.Sosabowski defended the coast at Largo Bay. The 2ⁿᵈ Rifles Battalion (from 1ˢᵗ Independent Rifle Brigade) was in reserve at Cupar, whilst the reconnaissance unit

---

[90] IPMS, KOL.1/DCNW/ 29 October 1940, app.1, p.1
[91] Field Marshal Lord Alan Brooke, *War Diaries* 1939-1945, edited by A.Danchev and D.Todman, London 2001, p.128.
[92] IPMS, KOL.1/DCNW/13 December 1940, App.1, p.1

was at Cares. Angus was defended by the formations of the 10th Armoured Cavalry Brigade (24th Lancers Regiment, 10th Mounted Rifles Regiment and 10th Dragoon Battalion) with the area east of Dundee held by 5th Cadre Rifle Brigade. The corps main reserves the Rattray Group was based at Rattray, Blairgowrie and Cupar Angus covering the Polish sectors' northern flank. If the need arose it was to operate in support of the main defence forces. The 3rd Cadre Rifle Brigade at Cowdenbeath, the 7th Cadre Rifle Brigade at Dunfermline and the 8th Cadre Rifle Brigade at Kirkcaldy formed the reserve on the right wing of the corps. The reserves could be moved up quickly by motorised columns (80 lorries in all).[93] Initial defence plans of individual towns such as Dundee were made on Bartholomews's town plans, onto which were drawn strong points, lines of fire, gun emplacements, barbed wire defences and road blocks.[94]

In the standing operational order no.2 for the defence of sub sector Dundee and Broughty Ferry (5th Cadre Rifle Brigade) an assault from the air was deemed more probable than one from the sea. The main task remained the defence of the port. Here the Polish forces had at their disposal the 1st and 2nd City of Dundee Home Guard Battalions (mobilised on the basis of 9th Battalion Black Watch). Various other British units on the brigade's territory were under the orders of the local Sub Area Commander. It is interesting to note, that one of the attached enclosures to that order provides exact addresses and telephone numbers of buildings where individual strong points and gun

[93] TNA, WO 166/128 Operational Instruction no.6, 4 February 1941; Notes on Army Commanders Conference at BHQ, 16 June 1941, app. I to War Diary for June 1941; WO 166/129 BGS Scottish Command to HQ Polish Forces ScCCr.S4/32620/G (Ops); PISM, A.VI.1/105, Defence of Dundee, General Operational Order no.2, HQ 5th Cadre Brigade, 1 July 1941.
[94] IPMS, A.VI.1/105, Bartholomew's Town Plan of Dundee as used by HQ 5th Cadre Brigade; PISM, A.VI. 31/1, Fortifications of Rosyth Naval Docks, 1940.

positions were located in the city. Similar plans were drawn up for St.Andrews and other main points of defence.

A major headache for the defenders was the need to strengthen existing and build new field fortifications, the former which being in a pitiable state and much outdated. Work begun on preparing gun emplacements in the towns and the preparation of communication demolition works should the enemy make a successful landing. A special Engineer Group was formed. Detailed plans were drawn up amongst others of blowing bridges on the main directions that the Germans would move along. For example it was expected that in the north the enemy would move along the axis Braemer – Perth and secondly along the Kingussie – Blairgowrie axis. It was foreseen that the centre of the main demolitions works would be on the Lunan Burn River, the lakes and on the rivers Tay and Isla. This would delay the enemy advance on the line Bridge of Cally – Blairgowrie. If time permitted, secondary demolition works were also to be carried out. The demolition of each object, mainly bridges were prepared in detail. These included line drawings of the object in question, the amount and placement of explosives needed to carry out the task. Thus for example the eastern end of the 16-yard long stone arched bridge on the river Black between Braemer and Rattray was to be blown by two 50-pound explosive packs.[95] Beach defences, anti-tank obstacles, well-hidden gun emplacements and pillboxes all had to be built.

An important part of the defensive system depended on the artillery and detailed dispositional orders were issued for artillery batteries and troops both on the beachheads themselves as well as those situated further inland. Their main task was to defend the ports and shoot up aerodromes in the event of enemy landings. Much had to be done. Lt-Col. Karol Maresch

---

[95] IPMS, A.VI.31/4, Demolition plans along the Braemer-Perth axis as prepared by Lt.Edward Kozłowski, 1st Engineers Company, 18 June 1941; General table of main demolitions.

commander of a troop of the 1st Light Artillery Battery wrote in his diary about the building of artillery emplacements and observation points in the defence of St.Andrew's in torrential rainfalls. His troop had a clear view of the beach in front of Links and the Bay of Eden Mouth. He wrote about the difficulties due to a lack of camouflage materials and wood. He was convinced that with the shortage of artillery available, whatever was had, should be used as a mobile reserve as and when necessary and not as a stationary force directly on the beaches.[96] The only enemy action seen by the defenders were as a result of several bombing raids either by single aircraft or by small formations, amongst others on St.Andrews on 25 October 1940 during which there were several fatalities and the destruction of part of the university. A few days later enemy bombs fell near the Kinkelness artillery observation post and along the road near Boarhills, fortunately without casualties. Not without irony, Lt-Col.Maresch noted that at the end of October 1940 after his troop had taken over its allotted section from their British colleagues, that there was a lack of observation equipment and had at their disposal only a minimum of signals equipment. Having had to return their vehicles, the troop that, according to plans from above was to have been a mobile one, became a stationary one. At the same time the demands made of it by its superiors grew, so much so that it had to cover a 12-mile stretch with 480 rounds at its disposal.[97] A major part of the preparations consisted of intensive firearm and technical training as well as exercises. From spring 1941 with the appointment of Lt-Gen. Sir Andrew Thorne as GOC-in-C Scottish Command inter allied exercises were noticeably stepped up and Polish

---

[96] Maresch Family Archive, diary of Col.Karol Maresch, entries for October and November 1941.
[97] ibidem.

forces undertook the training of various local Home Guard companies.

If the invasion were to side step the I Corps sector then it was planned that the corps would be used in a flanking attack against the enemy landing in one of the neighbouring sectors defended by British forces. In February 1941 the Polish sector was extended northwards to encompass Montrose. Defence plans were constantly updated and adjusted to the developing circumstances of the war. The invasion of the Soviet Union by Germany on 22 June 1941 decided the War Office that the erstwhile possible if not likely invasion threat to Scotland was much diminished and subsequently front line defence forces were reduced. The defence of Angus was taken over totally by the cadre brigades whilst 10th Motorized Cavalry Brigade was withdrawn to the reserves of I Corps and earmarked for expansion into an armoured division. Defence plans continued to be updated until 1943, though increasingly merely as a precaution and more practically as exercises.[98]

With the passing of the first threat of a German invasion during the winter of 1940/1941, the British suggested a reorganisation of Polish I Corp along British establishment lines. This was not favoured by the Polish command, which presented their own project based on the specific needs of the Polish Armed Forces in exile. Accepting the British project it postulated differing establishments of individual units with a higher percentage of officers. The reason for this was the specifics of operating an armed force on foreign territory with a surplus of officers above other ranks and difficulty in obtaining reinforcements. Following the signing of the Polish-Soviet Agreement of 30 July 1941, Gen.Sikorski had high expectations

---

[98] IPMS, A.VI.1/61, Defence Plan no.3 for the Fife Sector (1st Independent Rifle Brigade), 20 September 1942; PISM, A.VO.1/62, Operational Order no.1 Polish Support Group, 1st Armoured Division, 17 March 1943.

of bringing I Corps up to full operational strength with the aim of it taking part in the future invasion of the Continent.

In June 1941 it was decided to reorganise the I Corps along British lines. Because of it being continuously under strength it was decided to train each soldier in a number of specialities. The long-term aim was to create an Armoured-Motorised Corps. This led to emphasis being laid on the organisation and training of armoured forces personnel, which in future would allow for the creation of several large armoured formations at divisional or brigade level.[99] It was at this time that discussions took place concerning the organisation of an armoured division. The driving force behind this was Gen. Stanisław Maczek commander of the 10th Motorised Cavalry Brigade which had shown its worth in the September 1939 Campaign and then again in the 1940 French Campaign. In 1940 on Scottish soil it had been rebuilt for a second time with most of its officer and NCO's intact. Thus from the outset it formed in Britain, a badly needed battle experienced formation.[100] The 1st Armoured Division was finally established in February 1942 consisting of two armoured brigades and extra divisional units.[101] This division along with the 1st Independent Rifle Brigade formed the major operational part of I Corps. The newly formed 1st Independent Airborne Brigade was subordinated directly to the Polish C-in-C, whilst the Training Brigade, which had been formed from three of the cadre brigades, was earmarked to become the basis for the Polish Army Territorial

---

[99] IPMS, A.XII.1/48b-c, Report from briefing by GOC I Corps, Gen.M.Kukiel, 28 June 1941, p.2-4.

[100] IPMS, A.XII.22/10, Gen.S.Maczek's report to C-in-C Polish Armed Forces concerning the creation of an armoured division, 20 October 1941; KOL.1/DCNW/October 1941 Gen.W.Sikorski to Winston Churchill and Generals A.Brooke, J.Dill, G.Martel.

[101] IPMS, A.XII.22/10, Initial instructions concerning the formation of the 1st Armoured Division, 25 February 1942.

104 Wawer and Suchcitz

Command (administrative and training centres) in Great Britain.[102]

Until gaining full operational status I Corps was responsible for all Polish administrative and training centres in Scotland. On achieving the operational status it was to become an exclusively tactical formation ready for operations on the Continent. Gen.Sikorski was to be disappointed with the lack of adequate reinforcements coming from personnel released from the Soviet gulags. Thus to bring 1st Armoured Division to near full war establishment he decided to liquidate the 1st Independent Rifle Brigade and transfer its trained personnel to the former. In March a further reorganisation was initiated resulting in the inclusion of the 1st Armoured Division, the 1st (later renamed 2nd) Cadre Grenadiers Division, 1st Medium Artillery Regiment and corps units into the new Ist Corps. The armoured division and corps units were to reach combat readiness as soon as possible, whilst the cadre division and the remaining units were to reach combat readiness whilst the former were already on the Continent.

It was during this time that a sharp debate on the organisation of the armoured division took place. The War Office on the basis of recent operations reduced their own armoured divisions by one armoured brigade replacing it with a motorised infantry brigade. The Polish C-in-C, Gen.Sikorski and his successor Gen.Sosnkowski were firmly of the opinion that both armoured brigades should be kept. The reason for this was forward planning. Their intention was that the second armoured brigade would become the basis for a second armoured division. With the shortage of manpower the formation of an extra infantry brigade posed very real problems.

---

[102] IPMS, A.XII.28/3, Reorganisation of I Corps. C-in-C's Instruction no.370 of 20 March 1943 and GOC I Corp's Instruction no.3905 of 3 April 1943.

For this reason Gen.Sikorski and his successor believed that there should be an exchange of brigade formations between the Polish Army in Scotland and the Polish Army in the Middle East. This for various reasons, transport among them was rejected by the War Office.[103] Moreover, the War Office made it clear that if the Polish General Staff did not accept its *'recommendations'*, then the 1st Armoured Division would be crossed out from the order of battle of 21st Army Group. In the end the Polish authorities accepted, with obvious reservations, the demands of the British War Office.

On 21 September 1943 a new organisation of Polish Forces in the UK was established. Apart from those institutions and formations directly subordinated to the Commander-in-Chief, all forces were subordinated to the General Officer Commanding Polish Forces in the UK, Gen. Janusz Głuchowski. Its potential operational force remained the I Army Corps, now under Gen. Mieczysław Boruta-Spiechowicz. Having accepted British demands, the 1st Armoured Division was reorganised on the lines of one armoured and one infantry brigade.[104] From the remainder of the Division's armoured units was formed the 16th Independent Armoured Brigade which for the remainder of the war struggled to come up to full strength and supplied the

---

[103] IPMS, A.XII.1/78, Gen.K.Sosnkowski's meeting with Gen.B.Paget of 27 July 1943; A.XII.1/82, Minutes of briefing by C-in-C Gen.K.Sosnkowski, 27 August 1943; A.XII.22/95, Minutes of meeting at the War Office on 28 August 1943; A.XII.22/10, Minutes of conference held at the War Office on 31 August 1943 concerning the reorganization of the 1st Armoured Division.

[104] IPMS, C.84; A.XII.22/86 Command Organisation of HQ Polish Forces in the UK; Reorganisation of the 1st Armoured Division, 21 September 1943; A.XII.22/87, Reorganisation of the 1st Cadre Grenadiers Division, 21 September 1943.

combat 1st Armoured Division with fully trained reinforcements.[105]

The 1st Armoured Division brought up to strength with much difficulty finally reached combat preparedness numbering 885 officers, 15,210 other ranks and 381 tanks.[106] This included the first reinforcement intake. On its departure for the Continent, the Division operationally came from under the orders of I Corps, though administratively remaining part of it (much in the same way Polish 2 Corps in Italy, was the operational part of the Polish Army in the Middle East).

Meanwhile from July 1944 I Corps became a part of Polish Forces in the UK and its commander losing his erstwhile rights as senior Polish forces commander on the British Isles. His main task was to prepare for combat readiness the renamed 2nd Grenadiers Division, which in early 1945 was renamed 4th Infantry Division.[107] By the end of the war all its units had been organised and were undergoing intensive training and preparing the 16th Independent Armoured Brigade for combat readiness.[108] The latter depended primarily on the willingness of the British authorities to supply it with the required tanks and armament for operational use. This was not forthcoming and the brigade retained its cadre character. Such was the state of Polish Forces

[105] IPMS, C.171/I, Chronicle of the 16th Armoured Brigade; K.Jamar (Jan Marowski), *With the tanks of the 1st Armoured Division,* Hangelo 1946; M.W.Żebrowski, *Polska Broń Pancerna. Zarys Historii 1918-1947* (Polish Armoured Forces. An outline history 1918-1947), London 1971, p.410-411.
[106] PSZ. Vol.II, Part 2, London 1975, p.134; K.Jamar, *With the tanks...*, p.27-48; M.W.Żebrowski, *Polska broń.....*, p.413-414, 422-423.
[107] IPMS, A.XII.22/90, Organisation of an infantry division and armoured brigade, 6 December 1944; A.XII.13/6, Organisation and formation of the I Corps, Order no.150, 5 February 1945.
[108] IPMS, A.XII.28/2c, Formation of the 16 Independent Armoured Brigade, 20 March 1945.

in the UK at the end of the Second World War, numbering some 70, 000 officers, NCOs and Other Ranks.

At various times and in various circumstances this force had been an important supplement of the defences of the British Isles in its darkest hours of 1940 and 1941, subsequently providing an armoured division for the invasion of the continent and an airborne brigade which participated in Operation Market Garden. It also provided combat trained personnel as reinforcements, not to mention the various specialised intelligence and technical branches, which played a distinguished part in the clandestine side of allied warfare against the German enemy.

INDEX

Clarke, William 'Nobby', 53
Clinton, President Bill, 30
Colville, John, 59, 62
Conrad, Joseph (Korzeniowski), 36
Cooper, Josh, 54, 56, 57
Cripps, Sir Stafford, 61
Czerniawski, Roman (Brutus), 62-65
Dansey, Claude, 60, 61
Davies, Capt. F.T., 13
Davies, Donald E. 55
Davies, Philip H. J., 59
Denniston, A.G., 58
Dickie, Prof. 19
Dill, Gen. J., 103
Dobkiewicz, Maj., 85
Dolecki, able seaman E., 42
Dowding, Air Marshal Sir Hugh, 27
Dreszer, Gen.Rudolf, 93
Dubicki, Tadeusz, 56, 66
Dunbar-Nasmith, Sir Martin, 37
Dunderdale, Cmdr. Wilfred, (Wilski), 16
Eden, Anthony, 26, 29, 31
Erskine, Ralph, 15, 52, 54, 58
Filipow, Krzysztof, 79
Foot, Michael R. D., 28, 67
Foss, Hugh, 52
Gano, Col Stanisław, 16
Garcia, Juan Pujol (Garbo), 64, 65
Garlinski, Józef, 61
Gaulle, Gen. Charles de, 33
George VI, King, 12
Glabisz, Gen.Kazimierz, 93
Głuchowski, Gen. Janusz, 105
Gort, Field Marshal Viscount, 76